UNAFRAID

A BETTER BOOK ON THE END TIMES

MARC ARLT

"Unafraid is a book that every believer should take the time to read. It conveys ideas and interpretations that fit within the grand-architecture of Scripture far more accurately than the popular 'doom and gloom' versions of end-time theories. It leaves us with hope for both our own lives and the future of mankind.

The simple, conversational style together with the well-ordered thought progression makes for a very comfortable read, facilitating truths that all believers should be exposed to.

The book does not seek to answer all questions, but makes a very bold case for a better expectation for the future in God and His intention with us and this planet. It uproots illegitimate, fear-based ideas and beliefs that have crept into the Church and has systematically paralyzed us.

This book leaves you… unafraid.

The best is yet to come."

- Frans Du Plessis, Snr Elder and Overseer, Life Enterprise: Household of Faith, Durban, South Africa

"In this book, Marc provides empowering vocabulary, reasonable explanation and helpful co-ordinates to grasp what can be a complex, perplexing and very distorted topic – the End Times. He provides sound Biblical markers and exegesis that help us make "sensible sense" of what has been made overly complicated, leading to uncertainty, insecurity and fear, which is the polar opposite of what is intended for Christians living in the earth today. There is too much fear in the world today, including in the church, and Marc helps us to lift our heads above the inadequate and often sensational End Time theologies which only foment such fear. He provides biblical momentum for a victorious and hopeful sense of the future in Christ. "Unafraid" helps us to avoid some of the sensational "red herrings" that distract us away for the vital and engaging task at hand of extending the rule of God in this world based on the already finished work of Christ. The understanding and explanation contained herein are consistent with the prayer of Jesus – "Your Kingdom come, your will be done on earth as it is in heaven." This work is an invaluable contribution to the Body of Christ at this time."

- Peter Watt, Pastor of 3C Church, Durban, South Africa

"Marc's new book was a pleasure to read and I recommend it unequivocally. I say that because I have great respect for his commitment to the authority of God's word, having enjoyed many discussions with him during my tenure in South Africa. His tongue in cheek humor and wonderfully free blog writing style take the difficult and confusing topic of eschatology and explain it all in a fresh and inviting manner. His approach invites us to challenge traditional thinking without pressing us to believe as he does. I particularly appreciate his challenge to the church to understand the call of God in later chapters of Revelation to fulfill its role in addressing cultural and societal concerns of our day. Be prepared to have fear of the "end times" removed while being energized to take on a more passionate pursuit of God's Kingdom now."

- Phill Olson, Assistant Manager at Global Awakening's bookstore, Global School of Supernatural Ministry South Africa

"Here is a book that can change your entire understanding of "the end times" - in a good sound biblical way! I highly recommend it. Marc's easy to read writing style and clear line of argument belies his diligent research and sound exposition of scripture. Most important is his interpretative key: Jesus' worldview and teaching of "The Kingdom of God." Whether or not you end up agreeing with his understandings, scheme of things and conclusions, in reading Unafraid you will certainly have a better look at the end times. You will be healthily stretched, throughly enriched and empowered in your faith in Jesus and the outworking and climax of His-Story."

- Alexander Venter, Vineyard pastor of Following Jesus congregation, Author, theologian and church leadership consultant

"Finally, a book about the "End Times" for everyone! A book about "The End Times" that brings hope rather than induce fear and will leave you feeling empowered rather than paralysed. As news of natural disasters, war and suffering loom large over our world, there are so many people living with a sense of anxiety, dread or puzzlement about "The End Times". I wish I could give them all a copy of this book! In "Unafraid", Marc engages with various respectable theological voices on the topic of "The End Times" and presents it to the reader in an accessible, well-articulated, easy-to-read format coupled with his signature wit and thoughtful eloquence. This book is a considerable gift to us all."

- Jana Niehaus, MA Clinical Psych & MA Church Practice

"There are two key beliefs that provide the root for how a Christian lives their life on earth: Their understanding of just how much Jesus accomplished in His death and resurrection, and their understanding of the "end times". We have had a wave of Christian resources sweep the nations unpacking the riches of the New Covenant, and I believe we are now entering a new wave: A wave that unpacks from Scripture a hopeful viewpoint on the end times, and not one of fear and dread. It will take skilled theologians, writers and teachers to present this perspective, and Marc is one such skilled teacher. He is a young, modern theologian for a new generation of people. His ability to dissect key information surrounding Scriptural texts is remarkable, and in this incredible and faith-inspiring book he presents a solid argument that we as Christians can indeed be hopeful for the future of planet Earth, and actually contribute to this future in a significant way! I am thankful to God for people like Marc, and highly recommend this book and his teaching to anyone who needs faith for the future of our planet. Christians should be the most hopeful people on earth! And Marc's teachings can help you be so hopeful."

- James Preston, Radio Presenter, Preacher, Entrepreneur

'Eschatology that leads to depression is never good eschatology! Marc, in this book lifts the reader into a hope filled expectation of God's gracious rule and reign invading the earth with a glorious culmination of heaven coming to earth. Far from the fear driven pop-culture of apocalyptic teachings that disarm and disempower believers, this book wisely and effectively navigates the often mis-taught and misunderstood topic of the end-times. Marc's book frames the good news of the gospel and it's end-point excellently and unpacks the difficult texts that have produced much of the escapist mentality of the church. This is a thoroughly biblical view of all things to do with the end and moves the church back to it's original mandate of being a 'Kingdom people'. Timely and prophetic, I cannot recommend this book highly enough!'

- Julian Adams, Director of Frequentsee, and author of 'The Kiss of the Father' and 'Gaining Heavens Perspective'

Thanks to Cherise Vickery for the concept for the cover design. I love the idea of a red origami dragon and how it is a symbol for our beliefs - often they can be constructs of our own design.

ISBN 978-1-521-89808-6

Contents

CHAPTER ONE

Preface

Before I start I want to say a few things.

First, the End Times are contentious. You probably already knew that. But I'm not one to shy away from tackling a difficult subject—especially when there is so much at stake! Dietrich Bonhoeffer was a German theologian who said, "*The Church of Christ bears witness to the end of all things. It lives from the end, it thinks from the end, it acts from the end, it proclaims its message from the end.*"[1] What we believe about where things are heading, determines how we will live here and now which is why I feel very strongly about what I have written here. The majority of Christians I know are unaware that there is a viable option to the End Times books which line the shelves of local bookstores. My hope is that with this book my voice is added the chorus of many others who advocate a perspective on the End Times which is more hopeful, victorious, Biblical, and less fearful.

Second, one of the misunderstandings I have encountered when presenting the material contained in this book, is that it is anti-Semitic. I need to make it very clear that nothing in this book justifies anti-Semitism, nor should you reach the conclusion that God has it in for the Jews. I do not have an anti-Semitic agenda, nor do I want to sideline the Jews in any way. The emphasis in my theology is Jesus. He takes centre stage in the purposes of God, and everything else gets worked out from there.

Thirdly, some thanks are in order, as no book is ever the result of one person's efforts.

---

[1] Dietrich Bonhoeffer in *Creation and Fall/Temptation*, cited in *Dwell* by Barry Jones, pg. 35.

Thanks to Phill Olson for your insight and teaching on this subject which has helped me immensely. I consider you my mentor on this subject, and it's hard to know how much of this book is as a result of your influence. My guess is: a lot. Thank you for your time in reading this work and for your encouragement.

Thanks to Jana Niehaus for your deep friendship and generosity of spirit. It has been a great joy of my life to journey with you. Thank you for your meticulous attention to detail in proofreading this book—bringing your incredible skill and insight as a practicing theologian and an editor. Thank you for your friendship and for keeping me honest. I so appreciate you.

Thanks to Frans du Plessis for providing great theological perspectives and challenges to this book. It is certainly better for our lengthy discussions. I really appreciate your friendship.

Thank you to my wife Nicole and daughters Julia and Katja for affording me the time and space to put these teachings into book form. Girls, you are too young to understand it now, but may God grant you the grace to be faithful witnesses to God's alternative arrangement of the world. To my wife, thank you for being my partner in this adventure of life and faith, and for always being ready and willing to join me down the road less travelled. God knows I couldn't do it alone. I love you.

Finally, thank you to the elders and good people of Immanuel Church in Umhlanga, South Africa for receiving my teaching on this subject for weeks on end so graciously. Thank you also for challenging the content—this book is better for you. You have been my family of faith for 17 years and I dedicate this book to you all. May you continue to walk in courage and fearlessness into all God has for you.

CHAPTER TWO

Introduction

If I'm honest, I never paid much attention to the End Times.

The frenzy and hype around it just didn't hold any attraction for me — what with the latest news from Israel and the Middle East, some new scientific breakthrough in microchip production which was definitely going to be the Mark of the Beast, and scouring the Old Testament prophecies for clues of the end of the world. It all required far too much energy and time. Trying to keep up with it all was like a full time job and I just had better things to do.

Maybe that's why you're picking up this book. Maybe you've been a part of enough conversations, heard enough preachers on TV or in church, or seen enough book titles on the shelves in your local bookstore, to decide it's high time you have an opinion on this subject. After all, most other people seem to.

That's pretty much my story.

But for me it was more than just wanting an opinion on it. As a preacher, I *needed* to have a opinion on it. More than that, I needed to have a *Biblically informed opinion* that was gleaned from sources more credible than the latest Christian bestseller list. So I set off on a journey and what I found stunned me.

What you'll find in these pages are my journey to a sane, hopeful, Kingdom perspective on the End Times which is written with you in mind (whoever you happen to be). Each chapter is about the length of a blog post and casual in style. But don't let my cheesy humour deceive you. This content has been formed by hours of historical research, shaped by serious scholars (just go and check out the Bibliography), and careful attention to the Biblical text.

Important companions on my journey were a set of guiding values which give shape to my eschatology (a fancy word for the End Times), which I believe are important whatever form of Biblical interpretation one happens to be doing. Simply put,

I reject an eschatology which:

- Undermines the nature of a good God as revealed in Jesus.
- Creates a dualistic, postmortem Gospel.[2]
- Re-empowers a disempowered devil.
- Disempowers God's people as partners with God in His Kingdom coming on earth.
- Renders our present labour in the Lord pointless.
- Creates hopelessness for the future.
- Fuels fear.

It is my belief that much of what Christians believe about the End Times runs along these very lines, and I believe it is time for some serious rethinking around the subject. So instead, I propose a perspective on the End Times which:

- Expects God's Kingdom to come on Earth as it is in Heaven with increasing influence.
- Empowers us as God's co-labourers and powerful partners in this Kingdom.
- Renders our work in the Lord necessary, valuable, and important.
- Creates hope for the future.

---

[2] This is a Gospel, or Good News, which only comes into effect after we have died (postmortem). It is basically the idea that what happens on this Earth doesn't really matter because it's all going to be destroyed in the end anyway. What matters is that people get to Heaven. It is dualistic in that it gives us the idea that God is only concerned about Heavenly, spiritual things, and is disinterested about Earthly things.

- Stirs faith so that we press on to see more of God's dreams realised.

These are some of the guiding values for the task at hand. But before we dive in, let me make three comments.

First, any ideas we have on the End Times (including this one you hold in your hands) are only theories. No one can claim to have it all neatly packaged, and wrapped up with a pretty bow. Otherwise we'd have far more consensus on the End Times than we do. With that said, this doesn't mean every theory is equally valid. Some perspectives are more valid and faithful to Scripture than others.

Imagine a puzzle, where each piece of Scripture on the End Times represents a piece of the puzzle.[3] There is only one way to put the puzzle together in a way which makes sense. But if you've ever attempted a puzzle — especially a large one with many pieces — you will know that it's possible to put two pieces together which seem to fit together but actually don't, and only upon closer examination, when the correct pairing is made, does the initial error become clear.

The End Times texts are like that. It's possible to connect small groups of Scriptures together but fail to connect them to each other. It is also possible to connect Scriptures together which seem to pair well but when compared to an alternative explanation, offers a far better fit.

This is true not only of pieces of Scripture but pieces of history. A major part of the complexity of this particular puzzle is that it involves "outside" pieces — history not recorded in the Bible.

I guess it should probably go without saying but I believe what I have to say here makes the most sense of most of the pieces of the puzzle. If I didn't believe that, this would be a different book. But what I have found along this journey is that this particular theory does a better job of creating a coherent picture, bringing

[3] Thanks to Phill Olson for this illustration.

together Scripture and history with greater clarity, is more faithful to Jesus' Kingdom vision, and is able to connect far more pieces of the puzzle together than anything I've seen out there.

Second, you may hold to a different belief than the one presented here, and you may be challenged on these beliefs. My encouragement to you would be this: do not be afraid to question your beliefs. Sometimes we can be afraid to adopt a new belief around a topic because someone influential in our life (perhaps a pastor or a Bible teacher) taught us a particular perspective on the End Times, and to reject that belief would mean somehow rejecting him or her. One of the lies we have believed in Western Church culture is that we can only work together, love each other, and remain loyal to each other by agreeing about everything. This is a fallacy which has done much damage to the Body of Christ.

There is a better way.

A way in which we can hold to differing beliefs and still love and honour one another and work alongside each other fruitfully. It is the better way of gathering around relationship, rather than doctrine.

Finally, over the years I have encountered many people who find the subject of the End Times to be a source of great fear. The '*Left Behind*' series of books popularised one theory on the End Times through the medium of fiction which has since spawned a handful of movies, and has left many Christians so afraid of the days which lie ahead. And with each fresh political event in Israel, that fear is rekindled.

I don't believe that God's truth ignites fear. However, I do believe it is possible to misinterpret the Scriptures and create a framework of understanding which can create fear. But fear is not of God. If there is something we believe about God that creates fear in our hearts, we have taken a wrong turn somewhere, and we need to go back a few steps and ask for directions. If that is true of you, my hope is for this book to help you navigate an alternative route which moves away from fear and closer to the truth and the heart of God.

I hope you enjoy the journey as much as I have.

PART 1

A Kingdom Foundation

CHAPTER THREE

A Jewish Story

If you know anything about the End Times, you will know that somehow Israel is involved. Maybe you don't know how, or when, but you know they are connected with God's purposes for our world. This is undisputed by everyone I've read on the subject, and I'm not about to challenge it here. But *how* they fit in with God's purposes and *when* they fit in, is where there is a major difference of opinion. It is important then that I start with putting Israel in their proper place in God's plan of redemption, doing so in context with the Biblical teaching and the teaching of Jesus.

To do this we must begin at the beginning.

When mankind sinned and chose a way of independence away from God, all of creation fell with us. The tentacles of sin reached their way into every aspect of human existence and twisted it out of shape. In a hundred different ways we became partners with the forces of evil to destroy our world and those who lived in it. Because God is the Creator of this good world, he took it upon himself to redeem it and all who live in it. He would not allow us to remain captives to our sinful fate, and so he set a plan in motion with a single family: Abram and Sarai. Together, they would form the seed of a plan which would be played out over multiple generations with a single purpose:

Now the Lord said to Abram, "Go from your country and your kindred and your father 's house to the land that I will show you. And I will make of you a great nation, and I will bless you and make your name great, so that you will be a blessing. I will bless those who bless you, and him who dishonors you I will curse, and in you all the families of the earth shall be blessed."[4]

God's purpose was not to choose this family and to hell with all the rest, but rather to use this single family as his vehicle through whom he would bless, redeem, heal, and restore the whole world.

Through them, God would reweave the broken fabric of society.

However it may have been expressed both in times past and at present, at the heart of the Jewish identity is not a narrow nationalism but a missional call. God chose Israel not to save them alone, but to save them and then through them to save the world. The prophet Isaiah put it so wonderfully: "*I will make you as a light for the nations, that my salvation may reach to the end of the earth.*"[5]

The trouble was (and if you're familiar with the Old Testament you will know this happens again and again) the very people who were supposed to be part of the solution were also part of the problem. They failed in their calling.

God gave them the Law (at one level) as a means to keep them on track,[6] but time and again they lost their way, so God sent the prophets to get his covenant people back on track and move the redemptive story forward. God disciplined and judged them again and again which resulted ultimately in exile into Assyria and Babylon, with the result that the Abrahamic covenant remained unfulfilled. Not only had Israel beached themselves on the shore of their own unfaithfulness, but God's purposes for the world could not move forward. The blessing to the nations (promised to Abraham) had become stuck within the failure of Israel.

Now this is where things get interesting.

---

[4] Genesis 12:1-3

[5] Isaiah 49:6

[6] Galatians 3:24

Some think that Israel and the Law was a failed plan of God's. He tried it, gave it his best shot, but as it turned out, it didn't work. So he went to *Plan B: the Church*.

But do we really think God is this faithless?

I mean, having promised to Abraham through a covenant to use *his family* to bless the world, would God shrug his shoulders in the end and say in exasperation, "*Oh well... I tried*"? No way! God is true even though every man may be a liar[7], and God is faithful even when we are faithless.[8]

Ok, so if God didn't just move on to a *Plan B*, what did he do? How did he find a way through the failure of Israel without simply overlooking their failure but still staying true to his word?

Now that is a great question.

Into this story enters Jesus. When the Gospel writers (Matthew, Mark, Luke, and John) wrote about the birth, life, death, and resurrection of Jesus, they arranged the material with a particular agenda in mind. It's like they were trying to tell us something *as they told us something*. Matthew in particular arranges his telling of the Jesus Story in such a way to show us that Jesus is the culmination and completion of the story of Israel. Their story had reached an impasse but now God has made a way through Jesus for the culmination of their story. Jesus embodied the story of Israel and so represented Israel, and we could say was the quintessential Israelite.[9]

---

[7] Romans 3:4

[8] 2 Timothy 2:13

[9] Jesus was the perfect example of a faithful Israelite.

Matthew tells the story showing us how Jesus came out of Egypt[10] (just like Israel did), how he was baptised to fulfil all righteousness[11] (just like Israel through the Red Sea)[12], how the Father spoke the words of affirmation, "*This is my beloved Son,*"[13] (just like God did over Israel)[14], how Jesus then spent 40 days in the wilderness[15] (just like Israel did for 40 years). Matthew arranges the story in this way so we might see that Jesus embodied the story of Israel.

But Jesus was also faithful. In the wilderness Jesus was tempted on three occasions. When he was tempted to turn stone into bread he used a text from the Deuteronomy which was a text associated with the testing of the Israelites in the desert around the issue of provision — one which they ultimately failed to trust God for — but one which Jesus would not fail. He would trust God. He would succeed so that he could carry the Israelite story to completion. In other words:

Jesus was the faithful Israelite.

Jesus was not God's *Plan B*, he was the fulfilment of God's *Plan A*.

Where Israel had failed, Jesus would succeed. Where Israel had been faithless, Jesus would be faithful. He would be the faithful Israelite through whom God would fulfil the Abrahamic Covenant. At last the nations can be blessed! God had found a way through the failure of Israel without being unjust, and without being unfaithful to his word by sidelining them.[16]

---

[10] Matthew 2:14-15

[11] Matthew 3:15

[12] 1 Corinthians 10:2

[13] Matthew 3:17

[14] Exodus 4:22

[15] Matthew 4:2

[16] This is the heart of Paul's argument in Romans 3.

Jesus ultimately dies on a cross (which is the sign of cursed man[17]) thus taking upon himself the curse of Jewish disobedience,[18] so that the blessing of Abraham might reach the whole world. Thus Jesus brings to fulfilment the Jewish story, he brings to fulfilment of the Abrahamic covenant,[19] and he reconstitutes the people of God around himself and a new covenant and no longer around Torah, Temple, geography, or a national identity.

God's intent was never a narrow nationalism, but always a missional purpose — one which Jesus has fulfilled, and continues to fulfil through the Church. The Church, we must understand, does not replace the Jews. Jesus has fulfilled the Israelite story, has broken down the wall which kept the Gentiles out of God's original plan, meaning God's purposes continue to move forward in an all-of-creation-redeeming direction.

I understand this is a lot to take in.

My two big points to take away are:

1. If we understand the story this way, we avoid the mistake of thinking that God's choice of Abraham and Israel was a mistake to begin with — one which he remedied with the Church. It was not a mistake. Israel is not a failed Plan A. The Church is not Plan B. Jesus is the fulfilment of Plan A, taking the story in a cosmos redeeming direction.

2. We avoid the mistake of thinking that God now has a separate plan for Israel — as though he hit the 'pause' button on their story, started a new story with Jesus, and will at some point into the future hit the 'play' button, and bring their

---

[17] Galatians 3:13

[18] Deuteronomy 28:15-68

[19] Galatians 3:16

story to a conclusion. Truth be told, God has already brought that story to a conclusion, and God has done so in Christ.[20]

If you can understand how we arrived at this point, you can dismantle most of today's End Times teaching including the bestselling End Times books lining the shelves at your local Christian bookstore, because most of them are based upon an incomplete story of Israel which is awaiting a conclusion.[21] The truth is, Jesus did not start a new faith. God has continued the story which began long before the Jews were even a people, and has now swung the doors open for all peoples to join him in his mission and purpose centred in Christ. As Christians we need to understand there is a rich history to our faith which is connected to the Israel story, but this also means Israel's story isn't one awaiting a conclusion because it has already received a conclusion and a fresh beginning in Christ who has carried God's redemptive plan forward. This single idea will shake the foundation of most End Times theories out there, which is why it was so important for us to start here.

But this is just the beginning. There is another key foundation stone we need to have in place: the nature of the Kingdom of God, which we'll deal with in the next chapter.

---

[20] I need to say again that God hasn't sidelined the Jews. Their story might have reached fulfilment in Jesus, but it doesn't mean God is done with them. There is still a seat around God's table reserved for them – if they will accept God's invitation in Christ. The story from here on moves forward with *Jesus* at the centre, not the Jewish nation. This is the mistake Dispensational End Times teachers make.

[21] If you want to read a bit more on God's plan for the Jews into the future, check out the Appendix.

CHAPTER FOUR

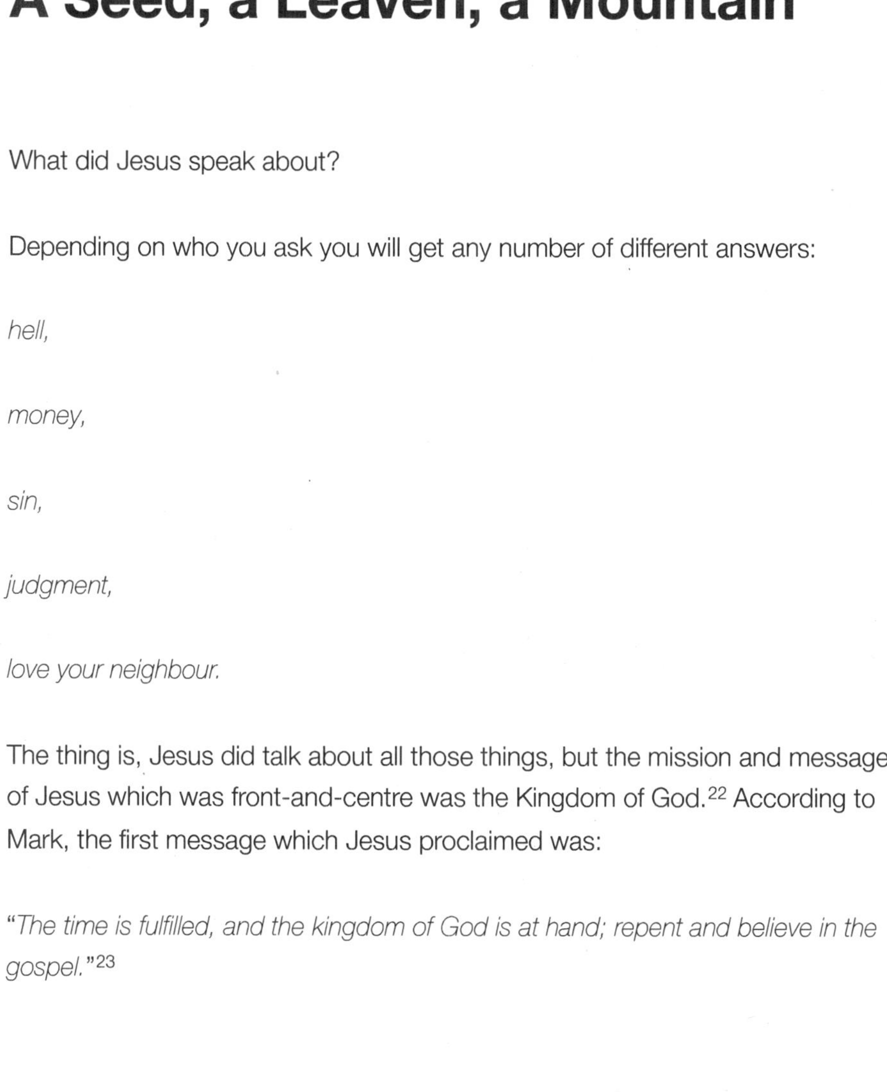

A Seed, a Leaven, a Mountain

What did Jesus speak about?

Depending on who you ask you will get any number of different answers:

hell,

money,

sin,

judgment,

love your neighbour.

The thing is, Jesus did talk about all those things, but the mission and message of Jesus which was front-and-centre was the Kingdom of God.[22] According to Mark, the first message which Jesus proclaimed was:

"*The time is fulfilled, and the kingdom of God is at hand; repent and believe in the gospel.*"[23]

---

[22] If you want to gain a solid foundational teaching on the Kingdom of God take a look at the teachings of Derek Morphew, in particular his book "*Breakthrough*".

[23] Mark 1:14-15

Here we have the announcement of Good News (Gospel) as the arrival of the Kingdom of God. The Kingdom was the Good News. The Good News of God's present and coming reign was good because of what it would mean for all people everywhere. It would mean peace, love, joy, freedom, reconciliation, healing, and redemption. A good word for this might be the rich Hebrew word *shalom*. This present and coming Kingdom would mean the reality of God's alternative arrangement of the world — an arrangement which would reflect his heart in every way.

Jesus made use of numerous stories (called parables) to explain his Kingdom message. However, contrary to popular belief, Jesus didn't tell these stories to keep his message simple for his audience, but precisely to keep the message of the Kingdom hidden — hidden in plain sight and accessible only to those with eyes to see.[24] Though his disciples had been invited into this inner circle of accessibility, it didn't keep them from frequently misunderstanding him or from frequently questioning him as to their meaning.

We might say these parables functioned as adjectives which described things which are true about the nature of this Kingdom, or they way the Kingdom worked. There are two key parables which are important for us in this present discussion on the End Times: the parable of the mustard seed, and the parable of the leaven:

He put another parable before them, saying, "The kingdom of heaven is like a grain of mustard seed that a man took and sowed in his field. It is the smallest of all seeds, but when it has grown it is larger than all the garden plants and becomes a tree, so that the birds of the air come and make nests in its branches."
He told them another parable. "The kingdom of heaven is like leaven that a woman took and hid in three measures of flour, till it was all leavened."[25]

---

[24] Matthew 13:11

[25] Matthew 13:31-33

So God's Kingdom is like a mustard seed, and God's Kingdom is like leaven.

While you hold these two parables in mind, let me add a third, this time from the Old Testament.

You might have heard of a man named Daniel. He lived during the time of the Babylonian exile. He proved himself to be a man of wisdom and skill and was therefore chosen to be an advisor to the king of Babylon. At one point the king, Nebuchadnezzar, had a dream which troubled him and which he was unable to make sense of. He summoned his wise men and gave them an impossible task: first to retell the dream, and them to offer an interpretation. Unsurprisingly, none were able to. Except Daniel. God revealed Nebuchadnezzar's dream to Daniel, as well as it's interpretation. He then stood before the king and said:

"You saw, O king, and behold, a great image. This image, mighty and of exceeding brightness, stood before you, and its appearance was frightening. The head of this image was of fine gold, its chest and arms of silver, its middle and thighs of bronze, its legs of iron, its feet partly of iron and partly of clay. As you looked, a stone was cut out by no human hand, and it struck the image on its feet of iron and clay, and broke them in pieces. Then the iron, the clay, the bronze, the silver, and the gold, all together were broken in pieces, and became like the chaff of the summer threshing floors; and the wind carried them away, so that not a trace of them could be found. But the stone that struck the image became a great mountain and filled the whole earth.

This was the dream. Now we will tell the king its interpretation. You, O king … are the head of gold. Another kingdom inferior to you shall arise after you, and yet a third kingdom of bronze, which shall rule over all the earth. And there shall be a fourth kingdom, strong as iron, because iron breaks to pieces and shatters all things. And like iron that crushes, it shall break and crush all these. And as you saw the feet and toes, partly of potter 's clay and partly of iron, it shall be a divided kingdom, but some of the firmness of iron shall be in it, just as you saw iron mixed with the soft clay. … And in the days of those kings the God of heaven will set up a kingdom that shall never be destroyed, nor shall the kingdom be left to another people. It shall break in pieces all these kingdoms and bring them to an end, and it shall stand forever, just as you saw that a stone was cut from a mountain by no human hand, and that it broke in pieces the iron, the bronze, the clay, the silver, and the gold. A great God has made known to the king what shall be after this. The dream is certain, and its interpretation sure."[26]

A remarkable dream with a remarkable interpretation, not least of all because we have the benefit of hindsight. Scholars generally agree[27] that the statue represents four kingdoms which were the Babylonian Kingdom (which was at that time ruled by Nebuchadnezzar), the Medo-Persian Kingdom (who would later conquer the Babylonians), the Greeks, and finally the Roman Empire.

Daniel then went on to explain the dream saying that, "*in the days of those kings,*" — in other words, in the days of those empires, during the time of the Roman Empire, "*the God of heaven will set up a kingdom.*" This kingdom, we are told by Daniel, will, "*break in pieces all these kingdoms and bring them to an end,*" however, "*it shall stand forever.*"

And, though it starts as a small stone, it will become like a great mountain filling the whole earth.

Can you see where I am going with this?

Three images: a mustard seed, leaven, and a mountain. In the first two, Jesus offers us an understanding of the nature of the Kingdom of God. In the third, Daniel gives us a picture of God's Kingdom which breaks into history by his sovereign hand (in the days of the Roman Empire — which is when Jesus was born), strikes those other kingdoms down, and grows to become a mountain which fills the whole earth.

---

[26] Daniel 2:31-45

[27] See for example, The Expositor's Bible Commentary, Jamieson, Fausset, and Brown Commentary, and Matthew Henry's Commentary on the Whole Bible.

When we put the three pictures side by side, all of them are in accord. They describe God's Kingdom as starting small but growing inexorably until it becomes a tree, leavens the whole lump, and grows to be a mountain which fills the whole earth. All three are in agreement regarding the trajectory which the Kingdom of God takes: it starts small and it grows.

To make my point even clearer, we should not expect God's Kingdom to arrive small, make small advances here and there, show some promising growth spurts, but ultimately fail to reach maturity, only in the end be trampled under the boot of evil. That is not the picture we get if these Scriptures are to be believed.

Furthermore, we have the prophecy about Jesus in Isaiah where it says, "*Of the increase of his government and of peace there will be no end,*[28]"

True to the trajectory of God's Kingdom, his government will know no end to it's increase.

Now, I have said all this because it is imperative that we have a belief around the End Times which is in line with our belief on the Kingdom of God as initiated, demonstrated, and taught by Jesus. What we believe about the End Times must make sense within this larger framework of the Kingdom of God and it's trajectory of growth. A key part of my own journey in understanding the End Times has been around recognising my own 'theological schizophrenia'.[29] I have since noticed it in other believers as well and it is a condition which has not been adequately diagnosed.

What I mean is this: on the one hand we speak optimistically around the fact that God's Kingdom is growing and advancing through healing, deliverance, social

---

[28] Isaiah 9:6-7

[29] This is a phrase I have coined to try and explain the way we can hold on to conflicting and contradictory beliefs. They can exist in our thinking and beliefs so long as they are held a sufficient distance apart and never brought into conversation with each other.

justice, activism, and a renewed connection between faith and work. In many places there is talk of a worldwide revival which has already begun and will not abate. Thousands of Muslims are being converted each month in the Middle East. Jesus is appearing to those far from him through visions and dreams. Through social media we are being awakened to a worldwide expression of Christianity which has recovered it's identity as salt and light. These are exciting days to be alive.

But then, when the conversation switches to the latest news on Israel our theological schizophrenia raises it's head as we talk about how this is just another sign of 'the End' and we should expect the days to get darker and the tide of evil to rise higher and higher and overwhelm the people of God who are waiting for the Rapture, hoping that God doesn't delay too much longer.

Something is wrong as both cannot be right.

Either the Kingdom is increasing and growing, or darkness is.

So how did we get here?

One explanation is that we have a fragmented understanding of the Scriptures and had no way to tell the Biblical story as a single coherent narrative. The result is that we have different Biblical subjects adrift without a solid mooring to a central theme (topics such as Israel, the Cross, the End Times, the Church, to name but a few). These are like pieces of the puzzle which make some sense on their own, but we have no coherent way of connecting them all together. This means we can entertain wildly divergent ideas from one subject to the next. I believe it is time for us to give careful thought to the implications of our beliefs on the End Times in the light of the overarching picture of the Kingdom.

The Kingdom of God must be the framework within which we fit our End Times beliefs and not the other way around.

As with the previous foundation stone, an adequate Kingdom theology is enough to dismantle much modern teaching on the End Times. If we start with the Kingdom the conclusion we will arrive at is not one which anticipates a darkening of the days, or a rampant rising tide of evil which will overwhelm the church to the point where God will rapture us leaving the world full of evil and ripe for his judgment. Instead, I believe we will see through fresh eyes of faith, a trajectory of the Kingdom of God as explained by Jesus, Daniel, and Isaiah as one of increase and growth as we pray *"your Kingdom come,"* and as we participate in it's forward momentum by the Holy Spirit until the day Jesus returns to fully consummate his Kingdom.

Now that's Good News worth sharing!

CHAPTER FIVE

Selah

At this point let us pause and consider what has been said, as these ideas are foundational for what lies ahead.

- Jesus was born as a Jew, and through his birth, life, death, resurrection and ascension, he carried the story of God's people to it's fulfilment. He was the faithful Israelite in whom the promise to Abraham reaches it's climax.
- Jesus reconstitutes the people of God no longer around a national identity, the Law, the Holy Land, the Temple, or circumcision, but around himself.
- The Kingdom of God spoken about in Daniel has come in Jesus.
- The Kingdom of God will continue to grow in influence. We should not expecting the light of God's transformative truth to be snuffed out by the darkness of evil and wicked people.

As you pause and reflect, here are some questions you might like to think through:

Have there been new ideas that have been presented to you in the last few chapters?

Is there anything specific you need to go back and read again?

Here are some further questions for you to think about:

Do you fear the End Times?

Do you think God's future plans for Christians include being afraid and defeated?

Do you think God's plans for the future centre on Jesus or on the Jewish nation?

What does this mean for your beliefs on the End Times?

Are you expecting the future to be one in which God's Kingdom is being pushed back and diminishing, or one in which it continues to grow in it's influence across the world?

Do you recognise a measure of 'theological schizophrenia' in your own life (particularly around what you believe about the End Times)?

PART 2

Matthew

Indirect judgment pronounced and enacted (Matt 21 - 22)

Direct judgment pronounced and enacted (Matt 23)

Specific details of the coming judgment (Matt 24)

CHAPTER SIX

A Prophet of Judgment

Jesus.

There has never been any person like him who has walked this Earth. Saviour. Lamb of God. Son of Man. Son of God. Messiah. Lord. Shepherd. Bridegroom. One wonders whether we could ever exhaust the multifaceted beauty of who he is to us.

Of all the titles I have heard ascribed to Jesus, one which doesn't feature often is the title of Prophet. Perhaps it's because Prophet seems too limiting a word and we don't want to give the impression that Jesus was 'just a prophet'. But seeing Jesus through the lens of 'prophet' is a necessary key to understanding who Jesus was and what he did and said.

Israel at the time of Jesus was under Roman occupation. The Roman Empire had vastly expanded across the Mediterranean region, and Jerusalem itself along with all Judea was under Roman rule. They were a nation captive in their own Holy Land. There was much hope that God would bring his promises to fulfilment and that the Messiah (king) would come and deliver them and establish them as an independent nation just as David had done in centuries past. They believed this Messiah would push out the Romans, restore the Temple, God's presence would return to the Temple,[30] establish peace, and rule on the throne of David as Israel's King.[31]

Jerusalem at the time of Jesus was a 3 walled city. The outer wall had been built by Herod who was the Jewish governor (or king of Judea), the 2nd wall had been built by Nehemiah, and the 1st, innermost wall, by David and his son Solomon which contained the Temple.

The Temple was the most important part of the city and indeed of the whole nation. It was the meeting place of Heaven and Earth. It was where sacrifices were offered, where healing took place, where babies were dedicated, and where God dwelled and met with His people. It was the single most significant site for all of Jerusalem and indeed for all of Israel. It was also the place which held all the records of personal debt. The Temple at the time of Jesus was the second Jewish Temple. The first one had been built by Solomon but had been destroyed by Nebuchadnezzar and the Babylonians and so was in need of rebuilding. This was done in part by Nehemiah, Ezra, Haggai, Zechariah, and Zerubbabel, and later expanded by Herod who made it one of the wonders of the ancient world. This is how it came to be known as Herod's Temple. This is the Temple which Jesus would have been dedicated in, and would have ministered in on numerous occasions.

On one occasion Jesus walks into the Temple:

And Jesus entered the temple and drove out all who sold and bought in the temple, and he overturned the tables of the money-changers and the seats of those who

[30] Whilst Herod's Temple had been completed by the time Jesus came ministering in Judea, it lacked the manifestation of God's presence which Moses' Tabernacle and Solomon's Temple had. God had not returned to the Temple.

[31] A big reason why Jesus was rejected as Israel's Messiah was because he didn't appear to do any of these things, and in fact his plan seemed to be heading in the opposite direction.

sold pigeons. He said to them, "It is written, 'My house shall be called a house of prayer,' but you make it a den of robbers."[32]

Jews would come from all over Israel, sometimes walking for days, to appear before God in the Temple in Jerusalem and to offer sacrifices. Rather than bring an animal with them which ran the risk of being killed or injured along the journey, they would buy an animal at the Temple. But because the Temple had it's own unique currency, you couldn't use your ordinary money to buy an animal and so the worshipper would change their money at the money changers, buy an animal for sacrifice, and then go to the priest who would make the sacrifice on your behalf.

On this particular day, Jesus walked in, overturned the tables of the money-changers and the seats of those who sold the animals, and for a moment interrupted the regular rhythm of Temple ministry.

For a moment he literally put a stop to the sacrificial system.[33]

If people couldn't change money or buy pigeons, even for a short while, they couldn't offer a sacrifice. And so for a moment the Temple's very reason for existence was called into question by the actions of Jesus. What Jesus was doing in prophetic action was speaking of God's judgment against the Temple and it's corrupt system.

After doing that, Jesus and his disciples left the city to stay in a town nearby called Bethany. The next day they are on their way back to Jerusalem when they come across a fig tree without any fruit on it:

In the morning, as he was returning to the city, he became hungry. And seeing a fig tree by the wayside, he went to it and found nothing on it but only leaves. And he

---

[32] Matthew 21:12-13

[33] Daniel 9:27. For further explanation on this verse see the Appendix: Daniel's 70 weeks.

said to it, "May no fruit ever come from you again!" And the fig tree withered at once.[34]

Jesus speaks against the fig tree and immediately it withers. It is a strange moment indeed. Why did Jesus do this? Was he feeling a bit cranky because he was hungry and hadn't had his cup of morning coffee?

Maybe.

But I don't think so.

What we have again is another veiled pronouncement of judgment against the fruitless house of Israel. How do I make this connection? Well, on a few occasions, Israel as a nation is referred to in botanical terms in the Old Testament, most notably as a vineyard[35]. In this moment with the fig tree, I believe Jesus is announcing judgment over the nation because they had failed to be fruitful in their vocation as God's vehicle of redemption and hope for the nations. This, unsurprisingly, is exactly in line with the prophets of old.

The disciples are astounded at what happens to the tree and Jesus responds to them by saying:

"Truly, I say to you, if you have faith and do not doubt, you will not only do what has been done to the fig tree, but even if you say to this mountain, 'Be taken up and thrown into the sea,' it will happen."[36]

I believe Jesus was saying more than 'prayer moves mountains' — though that is true — but when you are on your way to Jerusalem which is built on a mountain with the Temple at the centre of it, to speak of 'this' mountain (as opposed to 'a' mountain which would be more generic) being thrown into the

[34] Matthew 21:18-19

[35] See for example Psalm 80:8, Isaiah 5:1-7, and Jeremiah 2:21

[36] Matthew 21:21

sea is yet another way of declaring God's coming judgment over the city and the Temple in particular.[37]

Ok, maybe you don't agree with any of what I have said at this point. Maybe you think I'm grasping for straws to make a point. Maybe you're right. But stick with me anyway.

After the strange moment with the fig tree, Jesus and his disciples make their way into Jerusalem and into the Temple where they dialogue with the chief priests and the elders of the people. He is asked a few questions before telling them this parable:

"There was a master of a house who planted a vineyard and put a fence around it and dug a winepress in it and built a tower and leased it to tenants, and went into another country. When the season for fruit drew near, he sent his servants to the tenants to get his fruit. And the tenants took his servants and beat one, killed another, and stoned another. Again he sent other servants, more than the first. And they did the same to them. Finally he sent his son to them, saying, 'They will respect my son.' But when the tenants saw the son, they said to themselves, 'This is the heir. Come, let us kill him and have his inheritance.' And they took him and threw him out of the vineyard and killed him. When therefore the owner of the vineyard comes, what will he do to those tenants?" They said to him, "He will put those wretches to a miserable death and let out the vineyard to other tenants who will give him the fruits in their seasons."[38]

Ok, so now we have Jesus talking about vineyards and judgment, and even the Pharisees knew he was talking about them.[39] And it wasn't good news. Jesus was equating them with the wicked tenants in the vineyard, saying essentially

---

[37] In Daniel 2 a mountain speaks of a kingdom (God's coming Kingdom) so it is not too far to connect this mountain with the kingdom of Israel and it's imminent destruction. As you will see later in the book I believe this to be connected to the image John sees in Revelation 8:8.

[38] Matthew 21:33-41

[39] Matthew 21:45

that as a people they had failed in their vocation[40] and had stubbornly resisted God's attempts to bring them back on track. What then should this owner of the vineyard do, Jesus asks? Let their words ring in your ears as you read them again, for we will see in the chapters ahead just how self-condemning these words turn out to be: "*He will put those wretches to a miserable death.*"

He. Will. Put. Those. Wretches. To. A. Miserable. Death.

Woah.

In Matthew 22 Jesus then tells a parable of a wedding banquet and whilst many are invited by the king, none accept the invitation. So in response, "*The king was angry, and he sent his troops and destroyed those murderers and burned their city.*[41]" Again, keep these words in mind for they will be played out in agonising detail in the chapters which lie ahead.

My point is simply this, Jesus is everything I said before: Saviour, Healer, Lamb of God, and more. One thing which Matthew wants us to see as we lead up to Matthew 24 is Jesus is also a Prophet. In fact, he is a Prophet cut from the same cloth as the prophets of the Old Testament, calling God's people out on their sin, and calling them to repent or else judgment would come.

Maybe this chapter hasn't convinced you of that. If that is the case, wait until you see the next chapter.

[40] God had called the Jews to be a blessing to the nations (Genesis 12:1-3) and a light to the Gentiles (Isaiah 42:6), but they had become a nation which had fallen into the same patterns of sinfulness as the rest of the world: idolatry, injustice, and immorality. This is the basis of Paul's argument in Romans 2.

[41] Matthew 22:7

CHAPTER SEVEN

"O Jerusalem, Jerusalem"

After Jesus tells the parables of the tenants in the vineyard and the king and the wedding banquet, there are a few more questions back and forth from the Pharisees and Sadducees until we reach Matthew 23. Up until this point, Jesus has been declaring God's coming judgment in veiled terms (flipping tables in the Temple, rebuking the fig tree, casting 'this mountain' into the sea, the parable of tenants, and the parable of wedding banquet). But now, as he stands before the Scribes and Pharisees, he declares the coming judgment in no uncertain terms.

Maybe up until this point you've been unconvinced. Well, what happens next is going to shock you. From verse 1 through to 32 Jesus declares 7 woes over the Scribes and Pharisees:

"*But woe to you, scribes and Pharisees, hypocrites! For you shut the kingdom of heaven in people's faces.*" (vs. 13)

"*Woe to you, scribes and Pharisees, hypocrites!*" (vs. 15)

"*Woe to you, blind guides*" (vs. 16)

"*Woe to you, scribes and Pharisees, hypocrites!*" (vs. 23)

"*Woe to you, scribes and Pharisees, hypocrites!*" (vs. 25)

"*Woe to you, scribes and Pharisees, hypocrites! For you are like whitewashed tombs*" (vs. 27)

"*Woe to you, scribes and Pharisees, hypocrites!*" (vs. 29)

That's a lot of woes.

Woe is more than just a casual term. It is a term of denunciation. Jesus declares these woes over the religious leaders who have had a significant role to play in leading the nation, and he does it right in their own temple. Jesus then builds this to a climax and declares:

"You serpents, you brood of vipers, how are you to escape being sentenced to hell? Therefore I send you prophets and wise men and scribes, some of whom you will kill and crucify, and some you will flog in your synagogues and persecute from town to town, so that on you may come all the righteous blood shed on earth, from the blood of righteous Abel to the blood of Zechariah the son of Barachiah, whom you murdered between the sanctuary and the altar. Truly, I say to you, all these things will come upon this generation.[42]"

At this point, if you're standing next to the Scribes and Pharisees you'd be slowly but decisively inching yourself away from them. Nobody would have been wanting to be standing alongside them as they were on the receiving end of this Prophet's judgment.

Let's pay careful attention to these words of Jesus, for there has never been words like them uttered throughout the whole Bible (and never will be uttered again). Jesus says, "*all the righteous blood shed on earth from Abel to Zechariah … will come upon this generation.*" Two points are worth making.

1. God is going to bring about a judgment of all the righteous blood from Abel (the very first victim in Genesis) all the way to Zechariah, who was a more recent casualty of their violence-fueled religion. That is a lot of righteous blood.

---

[42] Matthew 23:33-36

This is a unique judgment in Scripture. It was a covenantal judgment which would come that generation for their stubborn refusal to act justly, love mercy, and to walk humbly with their God.[43] The nature of this judgment is unique and unrepeatable for any future generation. I will speak more about the nature of this covenantal judgment when we tackle the book of Revelation.

2. Jesus said who it will come upon and he gave the timeframe for this judgment to come to pass. He said it would come upon "*this generation.*"

In the Scriptures a generation is around forty years[44]. For the fulfilment of his words, Jesus' announcement of judgment would needed to have happened within 40 years. Scholars tell us that Jesus ministered somewhere around 27 - 33 A.D., so adding 40 years onto that we calculate a date of between 67 - 73 A.D., as the time frame for what Jesus had said would come to pass. The historical question we need to ask then is: did anything significant happen to Jerusalem in that timeframe? For those who are familiar with history, and Jewish history in particular, you will know the answer to this question.

Around 70 A.D. the Roman army marched on Jerusalem led by Titus (a Roman general who was the son of the Caesar, Vespasian), he laid siege to it, and by the time they had taken control of the city a few months later, the city had been burned, 97,000 Jews were taken captive, and 1,100,000 were dead. The Jewish population was decimated, their city was destroyed, and their Temple burned with fire. It was a time of intense suffering and unspeakable horror for those living in Jerusalem at that time, most of which we know from the writings of Josephus.

Josephus was a Jewish historian who had been living in a city which was conquered by the Romans. He was pressed into serving the Roman Empire by documenting their victories, and recorded them in a book called the Wars of the

---

43 Micah 6:8

44 See for example Numbers 32:13.

Jews. He writes of the conquest of Jerusalem by the Romans and says (I should warn you that some of his writings are graphic and disturbing):

But when the Romans went in numbers into the lanes of the city with their swords drawn, they slaughtered those whom they overtook outside and set fire to the houses where the Jews had fled, and burnt every soul of them, and laid waste a great many of the rest. When they came to the houses to plunder them, they found in them entire families of dead men, and the upper rooms full of dead corpses, that is, of those who had died by the famine; they then stood in a horror at this sight, and went out without touching any thing. Yet for those that were found still alive, they ran every one through whom they met with, and obstructed the very lanes with their dead bodies, and made the whole city run down with blood, to such a degree indeed that the fire of many of the houses was quenched with these men's blood.[45]

Eusebius was an early Christian Bishop in the 4th century who was regarded as an extremely well learned Christian of his time, and he said of the fall of Jerusalem at the hands of the Romans:

These things took place in this manner in the second year of the reign of Vespasian, in accordance with the prophecies of our Lord and Saviour Jesus Christ, who by divine power saw them beforehand as if they were already present.[46]

Jesus, functioning as a Prophet, spoke these things decades beforehand, and reputable historians attest to their fulfilment afterwards. This may be quite discomforting to consider Jesus doing and saying the things he did. Perhaps we have never thought of Jesus in this category before. We all have a tendency to hold onto a handful of ideas of Jesus which fit our particular set of experiences, which makes it difficult when we are confronted with the stark reality of Jesus as a Prophet announcing judgment. With that said however, we should not miss the way in which Matthew concludes Jesus' announcement of judgment:

---

[45] Josephus, Wars of the Jews, Book VI, Chapter 8, paragraph 5.

[46] Eusebius, Ecclesiastical History, Book 3, Chapter 7, paragraph 4. (http://www.newadvent.org/fathers/250103.htm, accessed 23 July 2015)

"O Jerusalem, Jerusalem, the city that kills the prophets and stones those who are sent to it! How often would I have gathered your children together as a hen gathers her brood under her wings, and you were not willing!"[47]

As a Prophet he announces judgment, but like a Mother he laments over the city and would rather suffer himself than have them suffer. The imagery here is vivid. There have been instances of a mother hen faced with a farmyard fire, collecting her young chicks under her wings to keep them safe. Sometimes she is successful and when the fire has burned out, you may find a dead hen with live chicks underneath its wings.

This is what Jesus wants for his beloved people. He will drink the cup of suffering at the hands of the Romans, and he wants for them to not have to drink it for themselves but instead for them to seek refuge in him — to follow his way — so that they didn't have to face it too.

This is the heart of our God.

Up until now we have seen how Jesus fits into the larger Jewish story which God was writing, we have understood what it looks like for God's Kingdom to come on Earth in an increasing and growing way, and we have seen Jesus functioning as a Prophet announcing judgment over Jerusalem (who will himself go ahead of the nation to face their judgment). We will now go on to address the specifics of this judgment which Jesus announced and enacted both directly and indirectly.

[47] Matthew 23:37

CHAPTER EIGHT

Asking the right questions

We pick up the story where we left off in the previous chapter. Jesus has just given the religious leaders a roasting, declaring God's judgment upon them, but acknowledging that he will go ahead of the nation to face their judgment himself at the hands of the Romans.

Having said all this to the Chief Priests, elders, Scribes, Pharisees, and Sadducees, he leaves the Temple and his disciples point out the Temple buildings to him, probably marvelling at their engineering and magnificence. Then Jesus, his head and heart still full of what has been unfolding over the last few days, says:

"*You see all these, do you not? Truly, I say to you, there will not be left here one stone upon another that will not be thrown down.*"[48]

Jesus may have made veiled remarks about the fate of the Temple a few chapters before, but here he makes it clear what will happen to the Temple: not one stone will be left upon another. The disciples are obviously quite intrigued, if not disturbed by this statement. If you had been there, what would you have wanted to ask Jesus at this point?

When will this happen Jesus?

---

[48] Matthew 24:1-2

This is precisely what they ask him: "*Tell us, when will these things be, and what will be the sign of your coming and of the end of the age?*"[49] It may not be immediately obvious, but if you look carefully you will notice they are actually asking Jesus three questions:

1. *When will these things happen?*

2. *What will be the sign of your coming?*

3. *When will be/what will be the sign of the end of the age?*

Jesus proceeds to answer these three questions in Matthew 24 through 25. But before we start looking at the answers he gives, we first need to understand the questions the disciples ask. What exactly were the disciples asking Jesus?

"When will these things happen?"

They are asking, when will the Temple be destroyed as you have just said?

"What will be the sign of your coming?"

When we read this question, we tend to insert our beliefs into the text and assume that they are asking Jesus the question, 'when will be your second coming?' But that is *our* question, not *their* question.[50] They had no idea Jesus was going anywhere. In fact, right up to the point of the cross, they didn't seem to comprehend what was going on. Despite Jesus' numerous attempts to convey to them the fact that he would die and be raised again, their understanding seemed darkened. Simply put, they had no concept he was leaving, which means they are not asking when he would be coming back.

---

[49] Matthew 24:3

[50] Sometimes we read the Bible as though it was written as a personal letter to us which leads us to make interpretive mistakes. The Bible wasn't written to us but it was certainly written for us, which means we should take care in how we read it, knowing that we are like outsiders listening in on someone else's conversation and from there drawing our conclusions on what God is like.

They were asking a different question entirely which had little to do with geographical (or spiritual) comings and goings. We can understand their question if we understand the framework within which they were thinking.

Jesus' favourite title for himself was the 'Son of Man'. This was a title he lifted out of the book of Daniel which was a significant phrase located within a key Messianic passage:

I saw in the night visions,
and behold, with the clouds of heaven
there came one like a son of man,
and he came to the Ancient of Days
and was presented before him.
And to him was given dominion
and glory and a kingdom,
that all peoples, nations, and languages
should serve him;
his dominion is an everlasting dominion,
which shall not pass away,
and his kingdom one
that shall not be destroyed.[51]

There are two characters who come into focus in this text: the "*son of man,*" and "*the Ancient of Days*". These are understood by most Christians to be Jesus and God the Father. If we take this to be correct, the prophecy of Daniel sees Jesus coming "*with the clouds of heaven*" (keep this phrase in mind as we will encounter it a few more times on our journey together) and is presented to God the Father where he is "*given dominion and glory and a kingdom*" — one which is everlasting and shall never pass away nor be destroyed.

[51] Daniel 7:13-14

When Jesus used this title 'Son of Man' a Jewish listener would have recalled Daniel's prophecy. The disciples' framework for understanding Jesus would have had strong roots in the book of Daniel and so when they ask him, 'what will be the sign of your coming?' they are asking the Daniel question which is, 'what will be the sign of you receiving your Kingdom from the Ancient of Days?'

They wanted to know when would Jesus become king?

It's not an unreasonable question since the Messiah was supposed to be Israel's true king. The question also had inherent in it the question of, 'when will we be freed from Roman rule?' If Jesus is king, then the Romans would be defeated as well, and they would "*serve him*" in accordance with Daniel's prophecy.

When we take a closer look at Matthew's text, and the question of Jesus' coming, the word used here for "*coming*" is the Greek word *parousia*. Tom Wright, one of the leading New Testament scholars of the 21st century, comments on this word saying:

If you were a Roman citizen, believing that Caesar was the rightful king of the world, but living at some distance from Rome itself, you would long for the day when he would pay you a state visit. Not only would you see him for yourself, but, equally importantly, all your neighbours would realize that he really was the world's lord and master.

Much of the Roman empire was Greek-speaking; and the Greek word that they would use for such a state visit, such an 'appearing' or 'presence', was parousia. ... And it's this word parousia which the disciples use in verse 3, when they ask Jesus about what's going to happen.

They speak of three things. Each is important in the long chapter that is now beginning, containing Jesus' answer to them: the destruction of the Temple, Jesus' parousia or 'appearance as king', and 'the end of the age'.[52]

[52] Tom Wright, *Matthew for Everyone (Part 2)*, pg. 114

So the disciples are not asking *our* question: 'When will the end of the world come?' or, 'When will be your second coming?' but *their* question: 'When will you come into your kingdom?' or, 'When will you appear as king?' (which, if you remember in Acts chapter 1, they asked him again in another way[53] — it really took them a long time to get it!).

"When will be the end of the age?"

Again, we must take care that we hear the question the disciples are asking, and not insert into the text the question we are asking. The disciples are not asking the question, '*When will be the end of the world?*' That is not the way most first century Jews thought. The belief widely held by the Jews was God's Kingdom would come on Earth, ushering in lasting peace and prosperity (shalom). The present "*age*" was one in which the Jews knew they were not completely faithful to God and were presently oppressed by foreign powers, and were hoping for an end to this present age and the dawning of a new age where God would establish equity and righteousness in his people[54], the foreign powers would be overthrown, and God would return and be their king. N.T. Wright again:

Within the mainline Jewish writings of this period ... there is virtually no evidence that Jews were expecting the end of the space-time universe. There is abundant evidence that they ... used cosmic imagery to bring out the full theological significance of cataclysmic socio-political events. ... What, then, did they believe was going to happen? They believed that the present world order would come to an end—the world order in which pagans held power, and Jews, the covenant people of the creator god, did not.[55]

The disciples are essentially wanting to know when the present arrangement of things will come to an end and God will put things right for his people.

---

[53] Acts 1:6

[54] Psalm 99:4

[55] N.T. Wright, *The New Testament and the People of God*, pg. 333

These three questions are really one question asked in three different ways. They are all questions which are connected to the expectations of the Messiah: '*When will be the messianic age when you will rule as king, overthrow those who oppose you, establish your Kingdom in Israel, and restore the Temple?*'

Without an understanding of the thinking of first century Jews, we can easily make the mistake of thinking their questions are the same as our questions. If we force our interpretation on their questions, the answers which Jesus gives will obviously be distorted ones since Jesus was answering their questions, not ours. This is where a large portion of the misunderstanding around the End Times originates.

But now that we have understood the questions, we can begin to understand the answers which Jesus gives to these questions.

CHAPTER NINE

Signs of the End... or are they?

The disciples ask Jesus 3 questions: When will these things happen? What will be the sign of your coming? When will be/what will be the sign of the end of the age?

Jesus begins his response to these questions:

"See that no one leads you astray. For many will come in my name, saying, 'I am the Christ,' and they will lead many astray. And you will hear of wars and rumors of wars. See that you are not alarmed, for this must take place, but the end is not yet. For nation will rise against nation, and kingdom against kingdom, and there will be famines and earthquakes in various places. All these are but the beginning of the birth pains.
"Then they will deliver you up to tribulation and put you to death, and you will be hated by all nations for my name's sake. And then many will fall away and betray one another and hate one another. And many false prophets will arise and lead many astray. And because lawlessness will be increased, the love of many will grow cold. But the one who endures to the end will be saved. And this gospel of the kingdom will be proclaimed throughout the whole world as a testimony to all nations, and then the end will come."[56]

This is the famous passage which has come to be known as the 'signs of the End Times'. This is the passage many call on whenever a new political event occurs in Israel, or some natural disaster strikes somewhere in our world, or when some new war erupts on a far off (and sometimes not-so-far-off) continent.

56 Matthew 24:4-14

We're told we should expect these things because Jesus said they would happen, and that they would happen before the end will come. And since we're pretty sure we're near the end these things should come as no surprise (so the logic goes).

Not so fast.

First, remember, when Jesus refers to the end, he's not referring to it in the way we refer to it. Jesus isn't saying, 'these signs will happen before the end of the world.' He is saying, 'these signs will happen before the end of the age,' which will make way for the age to come.

Second, rather than tackling these verses in isolation we should allow ourselves the freedom to read further in the chapter where it says in verse 34: "*Truly, I say to you, this generation will not pass away until all these things take place.*"[57] Recall from the previous chapter that a generation is 40 years which means the time for the fulfilment of "*all these things*" (which includes the signs Jesus gives here) is between 67 - 73 A.D.

So am I really implying that all these signs have already happened!?

Am I saying that these were fulfilled almost 2000 years ago?

That's exactly what I am saying.[58]

Let's consider these signs one by one:

False Messiahs

Many false prophets and messiahs appeared in and around the years Jesus ministered.[59] John Wesley, an Anglican who started the Methodist movement

---

[57] Matthew 24:34

[58] (Audible gasp)

[59] If you want to know why, you can take a look at Daniel's 70 weeks in the Appendix.

said: "*And indeed never did so many impostors appear in the world as a few years before the destruction of Jerusalem; undoubtedly because that was the time wherein the Jews in general expected the Messiah.*"[60] Based on historical evidence we can say with some confidence that this sign could have already been fulfilled.

Wars and rumours of wars. Nation rising against nation and kingdom against kingdom.

History will show that there has seldom been a period in history without war. The time leading up to the destruction of Jerusalem was no exception. In 40 A.D., there was a disturbance at Mesopotamia, which Josephus says caused the death of more than 50,000 people.[61] In 49 A.D., a tumult at Jerusalem at the time of the Passover resulted in the deaths of between 10,000 and 20,000 people. At Caesarea, contentions between Jews and other inhabitants resulted in over 20,000 Jews being killed. As Jews moved elsewhere, over 20,000 were destroyed by Syrians. At Scythopolis, over 13,000 Jews were killed. At Alexandria 50,000 were killed. In Damascus, a sudden uprising resulted in the deaths of 10,000 Jews who were killed within a single hour. In 66 A.D., 50,000 Jews were killed in Alexandria. Within a period of 18 months, four emperors in Rome were murdered and civil war broke out in the city of Rome. It was a time of great turmoil, and there were constant rumours of new rebellions within the Empire. Then, shortly before the Romans surrounded Jerusalem, there was civil war within Jerusalem itself.

It could be said with a great degree of confidence that leading up to 70 A.D. there were wars, rumours of wars, nation rising against nation, and kingdom against kingdom. We could say that this sign has already been fulfilled.

---

[60] Wesley's explanatory notes on the New Testament. (http://www.biblestudytools.com/commentaries/wesleys-explanatory-notes/matthew/matthew-24.html accessed 31 March 2016)

[61] The history offered here in brief summary can be followed up further in the writings of Josephus' Wars of the Jews.

Famines

The ancient world was no stranger to famines. Acts 11 records a prophecy of a famine which later took place during the reign of Claudius. In Jerusalem there was a famine during the Roman siege. Josephus writes about it in his historical account *Wars of the Jews*:

Then did the famine widen its progress, and devoured the people by whole houses and families the upper rooms were full of women and children that were dying by famine, and the lanes of the city were full of the dead bodies of the aged; the children also and the young men wandered about the market-places like shadows, all swelled with the famine, and fell down dead, wheresoever their misery seized them.[62]

This is another of the signs which could have already been fulfilled.

Earthquakes

An earthquake is not a natural disaster unique to modern times. When Jesus died, Matthew reports an earthquake,[63] as well as when he rose from the grave.[64] In 63 A.D. an earthquake destroyed the city of Pompeii. Then, just prior to the war on Jerusalem, Josephus writes of a storm and an earthquake:

[T]here broke out a prodigious storm in the night, with the utmost violence, and very strong winds, with the largest showers of rain, with continued lightnings, terrible thunderings, and amazing concussions and bellowings of the earth, that was in an earthquake. These things were a manifest indication that some destruction was coming upon men, when the system of the world was put into this disorder; and any one would guess that these wonders foreshowed some grand calamities that were coming.[65]

---

[62] Josephus, *Wars of the Jews*, location 6870 (Kindle edition)

[63] Matthew 27:51

[64] Matthew 28:2

[65] Ibid., location 5163

Again, we can say this sign could conceivably already have been fulfilled.

Tribulation

Jesus warned that a tribulation would come, where his followers would be hated by all nations and even killed. It wasn't long before it began. Saul, a Pharisee, launched an all out war against the Church, traveling from city to city to root them out and have them imprisoned or put to death. So severe was this tribulation in Jerusalem that the young church was scattered.[66] Later, Herod also got involved and had James killed and Peter imprisoned.[67] This tribulation intensified in 64 A.D. during the reign of Nero. One third of Rome burned to the ground, and Nero turned the blame toward the Christians:

Accordingly, an arrest was first made of all who pleaded guilty; then, upon their information, an immense multitude was convicted, not so much of the crime of firing the city, as of hatred against mankind. Mockery of every sort was added to their deaths. Covered with the skins of beasts, they were torn by dogs and perished, or were nailed to crosses, or were doomed to the flames and burnt, to serve as a nightly illumination, when daylight had expired.[68]

It was a horrific time for anyone who was a follower of Jesus. I do not wish to discount the persecution many Christians around the world face in our present day, but history is clear that this is another sign which we can say may have already been fulfilled.

Falling away, betrayal, hate one another. False prophets. Lawlessness increase and love growing cold.

John the beloved disciple wrote to the church of his day and said in a letter: "*[M]any false prophets have gone out into the world.*"[69] There may be many false prophets in our world today, but already there were false prophets not long after

[66] See Acts 8

[67] See Acts 12

[68] Tacitus, The Annals, book XV.

[69] 1 John 4:1

Jesus. Within Jerusalem itself, during the time of the Roman siege, false prophets arose to convince the people that God would rescue their city if only they continued to stand against the Romans. They were wrong.

Lawlessness within Jerusalem increased. Leading up to the war, and most especially during the war itself, factions arose with different agendas. Without a clear leadership and authority structure in place, chaos descended upon the city which resulted in much injustice, violence, and robbery.

Love grew cold. Some of the most heartbreaking stories are told by Josephus as he accounted what took place within the walls of that city:

It was now a miserable case, and a sight that would justly bring tears into our eyes … insomuch that children pulled the very morsels that their fathers were eating out of their very mouths, and what was still more to be pitied, so did the mothers do as to their infants; and when those that were most dear were perishing under their hands, they were not ashamed to take from them the very last drops that might preserve their lives.[70]

Josephus also writes of one woman who boiled her son, ate half and then fought with thieves over who would eat the other half. If these are not examples of loving growing cold, I don't know what is. Again, these are signs which we can say have more than likely already been fulfilled.

Gospel proclaimed throughout the whole world.

This is the verse which may seem to present the most difficulty. Usually it is used to encourage world evangelisation so that Jesus can return. Whilst we should not give up on this task, this verse, like the others, can be said to have already been fulfilled before the fall of Jerusalem (which Jesus referred to as 'the end').

How can I say this?

---

[70] Ibid., location 6710

Firstly, remember Jesus said all these things (which included the Gospel going throughout the world) would be fulfilled within a generation.[71]

Secondly, we should not consider "*the whole world*" to mean the whole planet, but rather in it's usage in the day, it would have been used to speak of the whole known world and most likely referring to the Roman Empire.

But can we really say that this text has already been fulfilled? Let us go straight to the Scriptures themselves:

First, I thank my God through Jesus Christ for all of you, because your faith is proclaimed in all the world.[72]

But I ask, have they not heard? Indeed they have, for
"Their voice has gone out to all the earth,
and their words to the ends of the world."[73]

Now to him who is able to strengthen you according to my gospel and the preaching of Jesus Christ, according to the revelation of the mystery that was kept secret for long ages but has now been disclosed and through the prophetic writings has been made known to all nations, according to the command of the eternal God, to bring about the obedience of faith — to the only wise God be glory forevermore through Jesus Christ! Amen.[74]

We always thank God, the Father of our Lord Jesus Christ, when we pray for you, since we heard of your faith in Christ Jesus and of the love that you have for all the saints, because of the hope laid up for you in heaven. Of this you have heard before in the word of the truth, the gospel, which has come to you, as indeed in the

---

[71] Matthew 24:34

[72] Romans 1:8

[73] Romans 10:18

[74] Romans 16:25-27

whole world it is bearing fruit and increasing — as it also does among you, since the day you heard it and understood the grace of God in truth,[75]

From these texts, Paul seemed to think the "*whole world*" had heard the Gospel. On the basis of his apostolic witness and the authority of Scripture, we could say this final sign might have already been fulfilled.

The point we have reached thus far is to show that the typical signs which many point to as present day indicators of the end of the world are in actual fact signs which have, in all probability, already been fulfilled. This is not to say these things (earthquakes, wars, tribulation, etc) don't still happen today, but they no longer function as signs of an approaching apocalypse. They are simply present day signs of a world that is not as God wants it to be. They are symptoms of the groaning of creation.[76] These signs spoken of by Jesus were the specific birth pangs which would signal an end of an age which would ultimately result in the destruction of Jerusalem, of the Temple and the sacrificial system, and indeed of the old covenant itself.[77]

---

[75] Colossians 1:3-6

[76] Romans 8:22

[77] Hebrews 8:13

CHAPTER TEN

Abominable Desolation

To me it seems the disciples got more than they bargained for.

After all, it was a pretty simple question: '*When will the Temple be destroyed as you said Jesus?*' Maybe they were expecting an answer like: '*Next Tuesday.*' You can probably imagine then the mouths of the disciples agape and eyes wide with shock and wonder, as Jesus continued his answer:

"So when you see the abomination of desolation spoken of by the prophet Daniel, standing in the holy place (let the reader understand), then let those who are in Judea flee to the mountains. Let the one who is on the housetop not go down to take what is in his house, and let the one who is in the field not turn back to take his cloak. And alas for women who are pregnant and for those who are nursing infants in those days! Pray that your flight may not be in winter or on a Sabbath."[78]

There is a lot here so let us unpack this Scripture by asking a couple of questions. First question: Who is Jesus instructing to flee to the mountains? He addressed it to, "*those who are in Judea.*" In other words, not to you and me.

Next question: Why should they flee? Because Jesus spoke about the appearance or arrival of the, "*abomination of desolation spoken of by the prophet Daniel.*"

So who or what is an abominable desolation? Some have connected this with the anti-christ, but I believe this is to make connections that are simply not there

[78] Matthew 24:15-16

to be made.

Matthew wrote his account of the Jesus story particularly for Jews who would have been able to interpret what he meant when he referenced the mysterious abomination from the book of Daniel. Luke on the other hand, was a Gentile doctor who compiled his account of the Jesus story from eyewitness testimony and historical sources, doing so for a man known only as Theophilus who was most likely not a Jew. So when it came time for Luke to speak about this 'abomination of desolation', rather than using cryptic references from the Jewish scriptures, he would need to use language that his Gentile audience would understand:

But when you see Jerusalem surrounded by armies, then know that its desolation has come near. Then let those who are in Judea flee to the mountains, and let those who are inside the city depart, and let not those who are out in the country enter it, for these are days of vengeance, to fulfill all that is written. Alas for women who are pregnant and for those who are nursing infants in those days! For there will be great distress upon the earth and wrath against this people. They will fall by the edge of the sword and be led captive among all nations, and Jerusalem will be trampled underfoot by the Gentiles, until the times of the Gentiles are fulfilled.[79]

Luke makes it clear that the 'thing' which makes desolate is not an anti-christ figure, nor some mystical spiritual power, but an army which would surround Jerusalem. Jesus' instruction to his followers was not to run into Jerusalem for protection as one might think of doing under the threat of an approaching army. Rather, they should take whatever opportunity they had to flee the city as it's destruction had been decreed.

A few verses later Jesus makes a somewhat cryptic statement: "*Wherever the corpse is, there the vultures will gather.*"[80] What could this mean? Tom Wright sheds light on this verse when he says:

---

[79] Luke 21:20-24

[80] Matthew 24:28

[T]he ancient world didn't always distinguish between vultures and eagles, and when the eagles on the Roman standards gathered around Jerusalem they would seem like birds of prey circling over a corpse in the desert, coming in for the final kill.[81]

It is a chilling image which Jesus describes to his followers. Knowing the story as we do from Josephus, the picture is astonishingly accurate. The Roman armies surrounded Jerusalem, carrying emblems of eagles raised on standards, and laid siege to the city which ultimately fell into their hands. But not before civil war and famine caused much death and destruction with the city so that, when the Romans breached the walls of Jerusalem, they came in like vultures picking off what remained on the carcass of Jerusalem and it's people.

Jesus wanted to spare his people this horrible fate so he instructed them to flee to the mountains rather than stay within the supposed safety of the city. It is interesting to note that a Roman general names Cestius laid siege to Jerusalem in 66 A.D., breached 2 of the 3 walls, and then for no reason at all, withdrew his forces:

It then happened that Cestius was not conscious either how the besieged despaired of success, nor how courageous the people were for him; and so he recalled his soldiers from the place, and by despairing of any expectation of taking it, without having received any disgrace, he retired from the city, without any reason in the world.[82]

This sudden unexplained withdrawal afforded any Christians who remained in Jerusalem to heed their master's instruction and flee the city, which they did, many fleeing to the city of Pella as recorded by Eusebius:

---

[81] Tom Wright, *Matthew for Everyone (Part 2)*, pg. 119

[82] Josephus, *Wars of the Jews*, book 2, chapter 19, paragraph 7

But the people of the church in Jerusalem had been commanded by a revelation, [given] to approved men there before the war, to leave the city and to dwell in a certain town of Perea called Pella. And when those that believed in Christ had come there from Jerusalem, then, as if the royal city of the Jews and the whole land of Judea were entirely destitute of holy men, the judgment of God at length overtook those who had committed such outrages against Christ and his apostles, and totally destroyed that generation of impious men.[83]

Thus not a single Christian perished in Jerusalem during those last days:

It is very remarkable that not a single Christian perished in the destruction of Jerusalem, though there were many there when Cestius Gallus invested the city; and, had he persevered in the siege, he would soon have rendered himself master of it; but, when he unexpectedly and unaccountably raised the siege, the Christians took that opportunity to escape.[84]

In short, the abomination of desolation is not the anti-christ but all signs point to it being the Roman armies which surrounded Jerusalem in 70 A.D.

---

[83] Eusebius, *Ecclesiastical History*, Book 3, Chapter 5, paragraph 3. (http://www.newadvent.org/fathers/250103.htm, accessed 23 July 2015)

[84] *Adam Clarke's Commentary on Matthew*, Matthew 24:13

CHAPTER ELEVEN

Tribulations

"For then there will be great tribulation, such as has not been from the beginning of the world until now, no, and never will be."[85]

This single verse strikes terror into the heart of many Christians – mostly because it has been hammered home by a preacher somewhere who believes this is speaking of the days to come. As you probably can guess by now, this isn't how I understand it.

The specific language used in these verses will help us in two ways.

First, Jesus speaks of a great tribulation which "*never will be [again].*" This means that there is no possibility of a double fulfilment of prophecy.[86]

Second, the fact that it speaks about a time after this "*great tribulation*" means that this doesn't signal the end of the space-time universe. There is a future beyond it.

The tribulation Jesus speaks of can be linked again to the horror of what took place within the walls of Jerusalem, first at the hands of the Jews themselves, and then at the hands of the Romans. What follows next is a brief description of some of the ghastly events which took place during the Roman siege and consequent invasion of Jerusalem. I include them to make the point that this truly was a, "*great tribulation,*" which can be said with some confidence has never

[85] Matthew 24:21

[86] See Appendix.

happened before, and will never happen again if Jesus is true to his word. You may prefer to skip these next few paragraphs.

Josephus describes for us what actually took place. After the city was sealed off by the Roman soldiers, he tells how the Jews committed terrible atrocities against each other, even horrific actions, such as cannibalism, which occurred during the famine. He narrates a vile account of a woman murdering her small son, cooking him, and then eating half of him, saving the other half for another time. Thieves broke into her house, driven by hunger and drawn by the smell of cooking meat, only to find that it was her son she had cooked. An argument then ensued as to who would eat the other half.

During the famine, some Jews swallowed diamonds and precious stones in hopes of escaping and safely carrying them to another city where they might have the means to make a fresh start. Upon discovering this invention of the Jews, the Roman soldiers captured individuals who had fled the city, cut open their stomach and entrails, for the purpose of searching and taking for themselves whatever they could find.

During the siege, while the Romans could not breach the walls of the city, they would capture Jews who were fleeing the city and crucified them within view of those on the walls of the city in an attempt to rob them of courage, in the hope that they would surrender their city before they too met the same fate. Josephus wrote there were so many who were crucified each day, they eventually ran out of space to put them.

These are just a handful of stories amongst many. By the time the war was over, around 1,100,000 Jews were dead. Jesus said that such a tribulation would never be repeated. One may object then in light of the more recent Holocaust during which a greater number of Jews were killed (around 6 million). It becomes difficult to compare these two events (how does one weigh the worth of a life?) as they were both massive tragedies which should not be minimised.

We might say that in the tragedy of 70 A.D. a greater percentage of the Jewish population were killed. Their Holy City Jerusalem had been razed to the ground along with their sacred place of worship, the Temple. Because of this their priesthood and sacrificial system had been put to an abrupt end. On all fronts it can be considered to have been a terrible and devastating loss.

I will leave you to reflect on these events for yourself and come to your own conclusion.

The point I want to make is this great tribulation spoken of by Jesus has more than likely already happened, in line with the other signs Jesus has already spoken of up to this point. This means at least 2 things for us.

First, we are not waiting for and expecting a day when Christians will be hated by all nations and all believers will suffer terribly. We don't have to live in fear of an approaching day of great tribulation which will sweep across our globe.

Second, this doesn't mean there won't be localised suffering or persecution for believing in Christ. Many Christians in hostile countries around the world continue to face persecution daily. This is still a daily and ongoing reality. But there is a vast difference between a great tribulation as a sign of the end of the age and localised persecution faced daily in the name of Christ.

In conclusion, we should not live with a hopeless perspective of the future, anticipating everything getting worse. We should not live in fear of the future, expecting the whole world to turn against Christians with the intention of committing mass genocide against all who confess Jesus as Lord. Instead, we should live hopeful, knowing that Jesus is Lord, and we are his co-labourers working to see his Kingdom come on Earth as it is in Heaven. God's Kingdom will move forward even in the face of opposition, violent though it may sometimes be. With God's Spirit with us, and the great cloud of witnesses cheering us on, we can press on knowing that gains will be made, even at times at the cost of our very lives.

CHAPTER TWELVE

Charlatans

"Then if anyone says to you, 'Look, here is the Christ!' or 'There he is!' do not believe it. For false christs and false prophets will arise and perform great signs and wonders, so as to lead astray, if possible, even the elect. See, I have told you beforehand. So, if they say to you, 'Look, he is in the wilderness,' do not go out. If they say, 'Look, he is in the inner rooms,' do not believe it."[87]

Jesus warns his followers that false prophets and false messiahs will come onto the scene near the end. His words to them? Do not be deceived. Under the kind of conditions which a siege brings, it was no surprise that leaders arose with promises of deliverance. This was, after all, the city of God — surely he would not let it fall into the hands of the 'Gentile dogs'?

We don't even have to speculate on these things. We know that false prophets did arise saying these very things. But none of those who made such declarations were speaking the word of the Lord and none were the true Messiah who would deliver God's people.

Jesus continued,

"For as the lightning comes from the east and shines as far as the west, so will be the coming of the Son of Man. Wherever the corpse is, there the vultures will gather."[88]

---

[87] Matthew 24:23-26

[88] Matthew 24:27-28

This verse makes it clear that Jesus is still answering the question his disciples asked him: "*What will be the sign of your coming?*"[89] What we have learned previously is they are not asking, 'When will be the sign of your second coming?' but rather, '*What will be the sign that you have come into your Kingdom?*' or, put another way, '*What will be the sign that you have received your Kingdom from the Ancient of Days?*' or even, '*What will be the sign that you are king and start your victorious battle against the Romans?*'

The disciples wanted to know when would Jesus receive the Kingdom and Jesus points them to the sign of vultures gathering around the corpse. It's not going to be hidden away or done in a corner somewhere. You are going to see it and hear of it far and wide.

We have already established that this sign was referring to the Roman army with the eagle on their standards which surrounded Jerusalem.

At the risk of stating the obvious: Jesus is not telling his disciples about a day thousands of years into the future when he would return again at the end of time. Remember, he is warning these twelve men (and those who would follow their teaching) not to be deceived by those who would try and lead them astray.

Matthew wasn't writing all this down thinking, '*Gosh, this is going to be really important information for people in two thousand years time…*' Matthew, and all those who were with him, knew that this information was important for them. Jesus isn't here referring to a 'second coming' but rather to a 'coming into his kingdom' as understood within the framework of the Daniel text.

This interpretation of the phrase the 'coming of the Son of Man' is in line with the way Jesus speaks of it elsewhere:

---

[89] Matthew 24:3

"When they persecute you in one town, flee to the next, for truly, I say to you, you will not have gone through all the towns of Israel before the Son of Man comes."[90]

"Truly, I say to you, there are some standing here who will not taste death until they see the Son of Man coming in his kingdom."[91]

From these two texts is seems that Jesus didn't think it would take a long time for him to, "*come,*" or to, "*[come into] his kingdom.*" In fact, some of the people he spoke to would still be alive when it happens. He obviously then could not be referring to something that would happen in the long distant future. When we stand in the shoes of a first century Jew, understanding the text of Daniel and then read these verses again, we can come to the conclusion that Jesus isn't talking about his second coming, but about his Kingdom being established here and now.

If we put the pieces of the puzzle together, Jesus is letting his disciples know that when Jerusalem falls into the hands of the Romans, this will be the sign that all he said was true, and they would know that he had assuredly received the kingdom from his Father as prophesied by Daniel.

---

[90] Matthew 10:23

[91] Matthew 16:28

CHAPTER THIRTEEN

Blood Moon Rising

"Immediately after the tribulation of those days the sun will be darkened, and the moon will not give its light, and the stars will fall from heaven, and the powers of the heavens will be shaken."[92]

Here we encounter the use of cosmic language for the first time, but before we jump to conclusions on this passage, let us remind ourselves again of the timeframe for the fulfilment of these signs. First, Jesus said these things would take place, "*immediately after the tribulations of those days,*" which means we are not to expect them to take place 2000 years after the tribulation happened. If we accept that the tribulation spoken of by Jesus took place in 70 A.D. then these cosmic occurrences would happen, "*immediately.*"

Secondly, 5 verses later (in verse 34), Jesus said all these things will take place within a generation. This included the cosmic signs. So according to Jesus these should have taken place within 40 years of him having spoken it.

These 2 points lead me to the conclusion that these signs have already taken place. But how could this be possible? Surely if something of this magnitude occurred we would already know about it?

What if we are not supposed to take this language literally?

If that's the case, what else could this cosmic language mean?

---

[92] Matthew 24:29

In the Scriptures, cosmic language is used in various places to refer to governing authorities and powers. One such example is when the writer of Genesis recounts the story of when Joseph disclosed his dreams to his family:

Then he dreamed another dream and told it to his brothers and said, "Behold, I have dreamed another dream. Behold, the sun, the moon, and eleven stars were bowing down to me." But when he told it to his father and to his brothers, his father rebuked him and said to him, "What is this dream that you have dreamed? Shall I and your mother and your brothers indeed come to bow ourselves to the ground before you?"[93]

Note how his parents didn't assume the sun and moon would literally bow down to Joseph. Instead they immediately understood it to mean that they themselves (as parents and those in authority over their family) would bow down to him.

Again, this cosmic language is used by the prophet Isaiah in his declaration of judgment against Babylon:

The oracle concerning Babylon which Isaiah the son of Amoz saw. ... Behold, the day of the Lord comes, cruel, with wrath and fierce anger, to make the land a desolation and to destroy its sinners from it. For the stars of the heavens and their constellations will not give their light; the sun will be dark at its rising, and the moon will not shed its light.[94]

This judgment was fulfilled in 700 B.C. but there is no record of sun and moon or stars being darkened. This again refers to the sun and the moon — the governing authorities of Babylon — falling from their place and no longer in authority.

One more example will suffice:

---

[93] Genesis 37:9-10

[94] Isaiah 13:1, 9-10

All the host of heaven shall rot away,
and the skies roll up like a scroll.
All their host shall fall,
as leaves fall from the vine,
like leaves falling from the fig tree.
For my sword has drunk its fill in the heavens;
behold, it descends for judgment upon Edom,
upon the people I have devoted to destruction.[95]

Here, Isaiah prophesies against the nation of Edom, and included in this prophetic declaration of judgment is cosmic language. Edom as a nation no longer exists, and the last time I checked the sky is still there, as are the stars. Which means it didn't roll up like a scroll, and they didn't fall from the sky. Instead, true to the Jewish use of cosmic language, it referred to the governing authorities and powers being toppled.

Similarly, Jesus' use of cosmic language was a Biblical euphemism referring to the powers and authorities falling (in his case referring to Jerusalem), and not in reference to actual planets or stars.

We use similar language today when we make reference to a nation 'rising' or 'falling'. We don't literally mean a country is being lifted up into the sky or sinking down into the earth — it is a euphemism, or a metaphor.

The point Jesus made is that this time would be a time when the world as they knew it would be in turmoil, and major authority structures would be toppled. He continued:

Then will appear in heaven the sign of the Son of Man, and then all the tribes of the earth will mourn, and they will see the Son of Man coming on the clouds of heaven with power and great glory. And he will send out his angels with a loud trumpet call,

---

95 Isaiah 34:4-5

and they will gather his elect from the four winds, from one end of heaven to the other.[96]

At the same time when all of this was going on, Jesus said a sign would appear in heaven. What could he have meant by this? One possibility is pointed out by Josephus (a *Jewish* historian who had no vested interest in proving the words of Jesus to be true) who spoke about the time leading up to the fall of Jerusalem: "*There was a star resembling a sword, which stood over the city, and a comet, that continued a whole year.*"[97] He goes on to list a couple of other strange occurrences and then says:

Besides these, a few days after that feast, on the one and twentieth day of the month Artemisius, [Jyar,] a certain prodigious and incredible phenomenon appeared: I suppose the account of it would seem to be a fable, were it not related by those that saw it … before sun-setting, chariots and troops of soldiers in their armor were seen running about among the clouds, and surrounding of cities.[98]

These are certainly strange signs, especially when we consider the one recording them was a historian, yet was convinced enough that he included it in his historical record. Perhaps these are what Jesus had in mind? It is not easy to say.

It will help us again to remember that, "*the Son of Man coming on the clouds of heaven with power and great glory,*" is the vision Daniel saw relating to the vindication of God's people, the defeat of evil, and the Son of Man receiving a Kingdom.

Finally, there is the picture of the angels sent out with a loud trumpet call to gather the elect. If this isn't the end of the world, then what could it be? Again,

---

[96] Matthew 24:30-31

[97] Josephus, *Wars of the Jews*, book 6, chapter 5, paragraph 3

[98] Ibid.

remember that Jesus said this would take place within a generation so that gives us a bookend on the timeframe for the fulfilment of this.

This gathering in is associated with the gathering of a harvest. However, this isn't a sign reserved exclusively for the future. Jesus spoke about sending his disciples as workers into the harvest fields which were already ripe.[99] Elsewhere John the baptiser speaks about Jesus in this way:

I baptize you with water for repentance, but he who is coming after me is mightier than I, whose sandals I am not worthy to carry. He will baptize you with the Holy Spirit and fire. His winnowing fork is in his hand, and he will clear his threshing floor and gather his wheat into the barn, but the chaff he will burn with unquenchable fire.[100]

John said part of the mission of Jesus was to clear his threshing floor (a reference to harvest) where he will gather the wheat into the barn (those faithful to God), but the chaff (those who were unfaithful — many of the Jews of the day) would be burned with fire. In my estimation, this is in line with what unfolded in those tragic days of Jerusalem's fall.

(As a side note: I have heard some Christians on occasion asking for Jesus to baptise them with fire. If I'm correct in my interpretation here, it's probably not a good idea and they should stop praying for that.)

I believe what Jesus says here about the angels with loud trumpets and gathering the elect from the four winds corresponds to what John sees in Revelation:

I saw another angel flying directly overhead, with an eternal gospel to proclaim to those who dwell on earth, to every nation and tribe and language and people. … And another angel came out of the temple, calling with a loud voice to him who sat

[99] John 4:35-38

[100] Matthew 3:11-12

on the cloud, "Put in your sickle, and reap, for the hour to reap has come, for the harvest of the earth is fully ripe." So he who sat on the cloud swung his sickle across the earth, and the earth was reaped.[101]

Some points to make on both of these text.

First, in both these texts (Matthew and Revelation) the word 'angel' is used. The word which is translated angel is the Greek word *aggelos* which means, "*a messenger, envoy, one who is sent, an angel, a messenger from God.*"[102] It is on occasion used to refer to people rather than to heavenly beings. In fact, Matthew uses the word *aggelos* in Matthew 11:10 to refer to John the baptiser. The point is that this word doesn't necessarily mean an angel. It could also refer to people.

Second, in both of these texts, the messenger(s) go out announcing the Good News of the Gospel and then a moment of harvest takes place where the wheat is gathered and separated from the chaff which is burned. This is clearly a moment of judgment, which is in line with Jesus' theme thus far.

I know many Christians might hear this and disagree: "*Surely this is referring to the future!?*" I can understand the objection. However, let us try and hear the text as they would have heard it, holding *their* hopes in hand (of vindication from their enemies, God's coming Kingdom of lasting peace, God's shalom on Earth) rather than *our* modern Christian hopes (of going to Heaven when we die and wicked people going to Hell). Jesus was not referring to an event which lay 1000's of years in the future. He was referring to the same thing he has been speaking about up until now: judgment upon Jerusalem.

This whole narrative fits together coherently, even if it's language is enigmatic to us, when we keep in mind:

1. The timeframe Jesus gave us: *Within a generation.*

---

[101] Revelation 14:6, 15-16

[102] Olive Tree Enhanced Strongs Dictionary (electronic ed.)

2. When we view the text through a first century Jewish lens: *How would they have heard it then?*

There is just one more part of Matthew 24 to speak about before we turn our attention to the book of Revelation.

CHAPTER FOURTEEN

Rapture

But concerning that day and hour no one knows, not even the angels of heaven, nor the Son, but the Father only. For as were the days of Noah, so will be the coming of the Son of Man. For as in those days before the flood they were eating and drinking, marrying and giving in marriage, until the day when Noah entered the ark, and they were unaware until the flood came and swept them all away, so will be the coming of the Son of Man.[103]

Remember that Jesus is still answering the initial questions of His disciples as to when the Temple will be cast down, what will be the sign Jesus has come into His Kingdom, and when evil will be defeated. Jesus replies here: *No one knows the day or the hour when this will happen*. He has given the timeframe of 40 years ("*this generation*"), but as to the specific day and hour, it is unknown.

When Jesus made reference to Noah, what do you think the Jews would have heard? Which notes does that chord strike? A major note would have been judgment. Judgment came in the days of Noah, and it came suddenly. No one knew the day or the hour. So again, judgment would come upon that generation and it would come suddenly.

Jesus continues,

Then two men will be in the field; one will be taken and one left. Two women will be grinding at the mill; one will be taken and one left. Therefore, stay awake, for you do not know on what day your Lord is coming. But know this, that if the master of the

[103] Matthew 24:36-39

house had known in what part of the night the thief was coming, he would have stayed awake and would not have let his house be broken into. Therefore you also must be ready, for the Son of Man is coming at an hour you do not expect.[104]

This is the text that has been used in many books and movies, in which crisis suddenly comes upon the earth as millions of people seemingly indiscriminately suddenly disappear (leaving their clothes behind of course): pilots, nurses, babies, motorists, are suddenly taken, leaving behind scenes of carnage, tragedy, and despair. All that awaits those who remain is God's fiery wrath being poured out on the earth on all the unrepentant sinners.

This certainly makes for good Hollywood, but is it the truth? Is the 'rapture' what Jesus had in mind when He spoke those words?

The rapture is a belief taught by many Bible teachers, and it is supported by 2 texts in particular — the one we have just read, as well as one in Thessalonians which we will get to in a moment. Let's start with the one from Matthew.

The point Jesus is making is not that people will be snatched up and away suddenly into Heaven. Rather he was referring to a coming judgment which resembled the judgment in the days of Noah. In saying this he was prophesying how senseless the destruction of the city would be. Whether at the hands of the Romans outside, or from the Jewish Zealots inside, death would come randomly. One will be killed and one will be left. One would be thrust through with a sword and one would be left alive.

Josephus bears witness to this interpretation when he wrote how the famine within Jerusalem during the time of the Roman siege was so desperate that people wandered about the marketplaces like shadows and would suddenly fall down dead wherever their misery seized them. He also wrote of how the brigands within the city would test their swords on those who were still alive, dispatching them to their graves, whilst others who were pleading for death were

[104] Matthew 24:40-44

refused and instead were left to be consumed by the famine. One taken while another left behind. Random. Senseless. Suddenly. And all under the banner of judgment.

Furthermore, if this text was referring to a 'rapture' when faithful Christians will be snatched away to be with Jesus in Heaven, why would Jesus use such a negative metaphor? Why say that he will come like a thief in the night? And why would he warn is followers to stay awake to keep the thief from breaking in? Is Jesus a thief? Are we to try and keep him out? If the 'rapture' is to be believed, surely we should be doing the opposite? If Jesus is coming, then stay awake and when the thief comes, open the door and welcome him in!

It seems to me that, far from referring to a future day when a 'rapture' will suddenly take some people into Heaven while leaving others behind, this text lines up with what Jesus has been saying thus far — the days leading up to the destruction of Jerusalem will come suddenly and with grave consequences. Those who are 'taken' then are not taken into Heaven, but refer to being taken by death either through sword or famine.

I said there were 2 passages which are used to support the 'rapture theory,' the second is from Paul's first letter to the Thessalonians:

For since we believe that Jesus died and rose again, even so, through Jesus, God will bring with him those who have fallen asleep. ... For the Lord himself will descend from heaven with a cry of command, with the voice of an archangel, and with the sound of the trumpet of God. And the dead in Christ will rise first. Then we who are alive, who are left, will be caught up together with them in the clouds to meet the Lord in the air, and so we will always be with the Lord.[105]

Firstly, note that in the context of this passage, Paul is referring to the return of Jesus at the very end. As Christians we believe Jesus died, that He rose again, that He ascended into Heaven, where He sits at the right hand of God as King,

[105] 1 Thessalonians 4:14, 16, 17

and that He will come again. This is what believers for hundreds of years have declared through the Apostle's Creed, first mentioned in the 4th century:

I believe in Jesus Christ,
his only Son, our Lord.
He was conceived by the
power of the Holy Spirit
and born of the Virgin Mary.
He suffered under Pontius Pilate,
was crucified, died, and was buried.
He descended into hell.
On the third day he rose again.
He ascended into heaven
and is seated at the right hand of the Father.
He will come again to judge
the living and the dead.

This is what I believe. Jesus will come again.

If he will come again, what will it be like? And what is meant by the language used here by Paul to describe it? To try and give some understanding of that future moment, Paul weaves together a few strands — a few different themes — to speak of the return of Jesus. He mixes his metaphors, and weaves them together to do his best at explaining things of which we are not quite sure.[106]

The first strand is the image of Jesus coming down from Heaven as in Exodus when God descended on Mount Sinai. The imagery is certainly there: The Lord descending, the archangels call, and the sound of the trumpet.[107]

The second strand is the imagery of Daniel 7 which speaks of being caught up in the clouds of heaven — only this time Paul sees not Jesus being caught up, but

---

[106] Thanks to Tom Wright for this exegetical insight and for connecting the pieces which follow.

[107] See Exodus 19:16-20

us.[108] The significance is that this is not just the vindication of Jesus, but *our* vindication as God's people, and our sharing and participating in his rule and reign.

The third strand is taken from the imperial imagery of the day. Paul lived in a world where an emperor might have gone away to fight a battle or make a state visit somewhere else, and sooner or later he would come back, and the citizens of the city would go out to meet him and royally escort him back into the city from where he would continue to rule.

In all of this, Paul is mixing these metaphors to try and give understanding to what that future day will be like. But the best he can do is weave together these images as signs which point into a mist. It will be something like God descending on Mount Sinai, something like the vindication and victory from Daniel, and something like the emperor returning to his city, being welcomed by his grateful citizens.

This then is the exact opposite of how this text is often taught. Rather than being a picture of Jesus' return to snatch us away, it is a picture of Jesus who is the world's true Lord and King, returning to his world to be gratefully received by all who expect him.

Matthew 24 ends with a reminder that this is God's household, to which Jesus would shortly return and sort out the disorder and maladministration within his Kingdom:

Who then is the faithful and wise servant, whom his master has set over his household, to give them their food at the proper time? Blessed is that servant whom his master will find so doing when he comes. Truly, I say to you, he will set him over all his possessions. But if that wicked servant says to himself, 'My master is delayed,' and begins to beat his fellow servants and eats and drinks with

[108] I realise there may be some confusion here. The application of this text in Daniel to Jesus is one which I believe is rooted in the historical events of 70 A.D. (i.e. in our past). It's present application as to the people of God as I am using it here, is still to be realised in our future.

drunkards, the master of that servant will come on a day when he does not expect him and at an hour he does not know and will cut him in pieces and put him with the hypocrites. In that place there will be weeping and gnashing of teeth.[109]

This is how chapter 24 ends. It is a warning spoken to his disciples but also beyond them to the religious leaders of the day who have been set as overseers of God's people (or household). Jesus warns that he will come with decisive judgment which will result in the unfaithful being cut off. He speaks about being cut in pieces, put with the hypocrites, in a place where there will be weeping and gnashing of teeth. There is no reason for us to assume that this is a moment of final judgment or that this is 'Hell,' since Jesus doesn't actually use that word here. It is more likely referring to the brutal result of a war against the Romans which comes as a result of the rebellion of the Jews against God.

In Matthew 25 Jesus gives two further parables (along the same lines as this one here) before finally making mention of the very end — the final judgment of all nations. This is the only place in these two chapters where Jesus spoke about the end as we refer to it. Until now, everything that Jesus has said, would have been fulfilled within a generation, true to His words.

[109] Matthew 24:45-51

CHAPTER FIFTEEN

Selah

If what I have been saying until now is new to you, then I know it is a lot to take in. The effort involved in rethinking one's beliefs should not be underestimated, so let's take a moment to pause and look back over the ground we have covered thus far:

- In Matthew chapters 21 to 23 Jesus announced judgment upon Jerusalem and it's leaders with increasing clarity and directness, doing so in both word and action.
- When the disciples asked Jesus about the sign of His coming, they were not referring to his second coming, but to the coming spoken about in Daniel 7 which is an appearing before God the Father to receive a Kingdom.
- When the disciples asked Jesus about the end of the age, they were not referring to the end of the space-time world.
- The abomination of desolation was not the anti-christ, but the Roman armies which surrounded Jerusalem in 70 A.D.
- The great tribulation referred to the time of intense difficulty and trouble within Jerusalem leading up to it's final destruction.
- The cosmic language made use of by Jesus, was not literal but metaphorical and referred to the toppling of governing authorities.
- The verses in Matthew supposedly speaking of a 'rapture' are better understood to coincide with the senseless and brutal killing which took place within Jerusalem during the time of the war.
- The verses in Thessalonians supposedly referring to a 'rapture' are referring to the return of Jesus *to the Earth*, rather than a snatching away of believers into Heaven.

- In Matthew 24:34 Jesus said that all these things would take place within a generation, which leads us to believe that all this took place with the fall of Jerusalem at the hands of the Romans in 70 A.D.

One may ask the question at this point, "*Well why didn't Jesus speak more openly about these things? Why all this hidden, mysterious, code language? If he intended his words to refer to Rome and Jerusalem, why didn't he just come out and say it?*"

That's a good question.

Perhaps there are two reasons.

First, what if Jesus *was* speaking openly? What if all the things he said were common understanding in his day? What if Daniel 7 was a text everyone was talking about, and therefore to make reference to the coming of the Son of Man was immediately connected with the hopes and dreams of liberation at the hands of the Messiah? It may be enigmatic to us, but it wouldn't have been to them.

Second, understand that if one lived in apartheid South Africa, you didn't want to be found in possession of a document which spoke about the imminent overthrow and destruction of that present government. The same would have been true in Nazi Germany. You didn't want to be found in possession of material which pointed to the vindication of the Jews and the toppling of the authorities. This is part of the reason why such language is used. The early churches in possession of such material would have been in great danger operating, as they very often did, under the noses of the Roman authorities. We will encounter this language again in the book of Revelation where we shall now turn.

Some questions for reflection:

How has your idea of Jesus shifted? Can you see him functioning as a prophetic voice against the waywardness of God's covenant people?

How have you previously understood the questions of the disciples at the beginning of Matthew 24? How has this changed?

What do you think was the significance of the destruction of Jerusalem in 70 A.D.?

Do you think this is what Jesus was referring to in Matthew 24?

If Matthew 24 has already been fulfilled, how does it change your perspective on the End Times? What things can you let go of, and what new things can you embrace?

PART 3

Revelation

Revelation of Jesus (Rev 1)

Letters to the Seven Churches (Rev 2 - 3:22)

Judgment #1: The Seven Seals (Rev 4:1 - 8:5)

Judgment #2: The Seven Trumpets (Rev 8:6 - 11:19)

Judgment #3: The Seven Thunders (Rev 10)

Vision of the Dragon, Beasts, and the Lamb (Rev 12 - 14)

Judgment #4: The Seven Bowls of Wrath (Rev 15 - 16)

The Whore of Babylon (Rev 17 - 19:21)

The New Heavens and New Earth (Rev 20:1 - 22:11)

The Epilogue (Rev 22:12-21)

CHAPTER SIXTEEN

Apocalyptic Literature

For most people Revelation is the most mysterious, intimidating, and fearful book in the Bible, and probably the one we avoid the most. It's filled with terrifying images of beasts and dragons, whores and devils, plagues, saints, angels, locusts, destruction, and ultimate renewal. These fantasy visions are the hallmark of Revelation and make it a book quite unlike any other. So where do we even start to interpret it?

First, we must understand what form and style the writing takes. One very helpful and important method of interpreting the Bible is starting with an understanding of what literary genre we are reading. Are we reading history? Narrative? Law? Poetry? Because each different style will inform the way you read and interpret it.

For example, if we open the book of Psalms we encounter poetry and song. If we open Proverbs we meet wisdom and wise sayings. If we open Chronicles we read history. If we read the Gospels we encounter story or narrative. Within some books the style changes. In the prophets for example, you have a mixture of history and poetry.

This is important because if we come to the Psalms looking to read it like a history book, we will find ourselves in trouble. Whilst there are some historic facts woven into the fabric of the poems, the task of the author wasn't to record history, it was to give expression to emotion through metaphor and poetry. We must therefore read and interpret it with this in mind.

When we come to the book of Revelation, we encounter a literary genre all of it's own. It is written in the style called 'apocalyptic literature'.

The word apocalyptic is an English translation of the Greek word which means 'to reveal'. Apocalyptic literature gives us, "*divine revelations, disclosing … states of affairs not ordinarily made known to humans.*"[110] The way it does so is through fantastic visions which differ from what we find in typical prophetic writings in one key way. Whereas prophecy makes use of ordinary metaphors such as a pot tilted from the north, or a sword sweeping across a nation, or a lamb being led to the slaughter, apocalyptic literature makes use of fantasy images: that of dragons with multiple heads, and beasts that arise out of the sea, and locusts with the appearance of horses with the face of a man and hair like a woman.

This form of literature served a specific purpose in the first century. During times of tribulation and hardship for God's people this form of language encouraged and sustained God's people:

Scholars debate the origins of apocalyptic theology and literature, but its basic function seems fairly clear: to sustain the people of God, especially in times of crisis, particularly evil and oppression.[111]

N.T. Wright observes that this form of literature was the, "*Subversive literature of oppressed groups.*"[112]

[T]here is no justification for seeing 'apocalyptic' as necessarily speaking of the 'end of the world' in a literally cosmic sense. … The great bulk of apocalyptic writing does not suggest that the space-time universe is evil, and does not look for it to come to an end. An end to the present world order, yes … The end of space-time world, no.[113]

---

[110] N.T. Wright, *New Testament and the People of God*, pg. 281.

[111] Michael Gorman, *Reading Revelation Responsibly*, location 498 (Kindle edition)

[112] N.T. Wright, *New Testament and the People of God*, pg. 288

[113] Ibid., pg. 299.

This means that Revelation isn't referencing the end of the space-time universe as though all physical matter would be destroyed. Rather, John and his readers were looking for the end of the present age where evil was triumphant and God's people were oppressed and persecuted.

Richard Horsley contends that "[f]ar from looking for the end of the world, they [Jewish apocalyptic writers] were looking for the end of empire. And far from living under the shadow of an anticipated cosmic dissolution, they looked for the renewal of the earth on which a humane societal life could be renewed."[114]

In light of this, we would make a big mistake if we interpreted this book literally — the same kind of mistake we would make if we read the Psalms literally and didn't take into account the language of metaphor and poetry. We are therefore not to expect actual dragons with multiple horns, or beasts, or locusts with tails like scorpions and breastplates of iron. These are fantasy images which represent something else.[115]

Secondly, when we read Revelation we must understand both the timing, and the chronology of this book.

First, the timing of this book is important. John received these visions because God wanted to show him, "*the things that must soon take place.*"[116] John was told to expect these things to take place soon — in other words not more than 2000 years later. Later in the book, John is told, "*Do not seal up the words of the prophecy of this book, for the time is near.*"[117] At the end of the Biblical book which bears his name,[118] Daniel is told to seal up the words of the prophecy until

[114] Michael Gorman, *Reading Revelation Responsibly*, location 508 (Kindle edition)

[115] Ironically, even those who teach Revelation literally understand this concept as they translate locusts as attack helicopters or other such things.

[116] Revelation 1:1

[117] Revelation 22:10

[118] Daniel 12:4

the time of the end. His words were fulfilled almost 500 years afterwards. The implication is that John should not seal these words up because they would be fulfilled soon (in other words in a timeframe less than that of Daniel's).

These two texts provide us with bookends on either side of the book of Revelation indicating when these things would take place: "*soon*" and the time is "*near*".

Second, when it comes to the chronology of the book, we must understand that the images and visions recorded by John are not chronological. In other words, just because something comes later in the book, it doesn't mean it chronologically happened after what preceded it.

Take a symphonic orchestra as an example.[119] The composer spends hours writing down the melody for the clarinets, and when they are done he moves on to write the sequence for the cellos, and when they are done he moves on to write the melody line for the oboes. But he doesn't intend them to be played one after the other — the composer intends for them to be played simultaneously together. And though it took him hours to write each part down in order, when each instrument plays their part together, it lasts only a few minutes.

Something like that is happening in Revelation. There are parts of the text which follow one after the other, but are actually unfolding simultaneously in time and history. At other times the text gives us the perspective of something from earth and then things shift and we get the same event but this time from the perspective of heaven. All this must be kept in mind as we wade into it's pages.

Finally, we must account for the dating of the book. If this book was authored after 70 A.D. then Revelation couldn't be referring to the fall of Jerusalem as Jesus had been doing in Matthew 24. If however, his writings were written pre-70 A.D., then it is possible that John is seeing something about the destruction of Jerusalem. I believe John wrote this book sometime between 65

[119] Thanks to Tom Wright for another great illustration.

and 70 A.D. There is some disagreement amongst scholars on this but it seems to me there is strong evidence to support the dating of this book in that period.[120]

With those introductory comments made, let us take our first steps into these mysterious waters.

[120] See Appendix: When was the book of Revelation written?

CHAPTER SEVENTEEN

The Revelation of... Jesus

Whatever we are to say about Revelation, and whatever images come to mind when we speak of it, we would be far from the mark if we did not begin by saying that this is a book about Jesus. It isn't about monsters or beasts or false prophets or harlots — it is about Jesus. In particular, it is about his Lordship, his judgments, his bride, and his future world. The opening words of the book read: "*The revelation of Jesus Christ...*[121]"

A few verses later:

[I saw] one like a son of man, clothed with a long robe and with a golden sash around his chest. The hairs of his head were white, like white wool, like snow. His eyes were like a flame of fire, his feet were like burnished bronze, refined in a furnace, and his voice was like the roar of many waters. In his right hand he held seven stars, from his mouth came a sharp two-edged sword, and his face was like the sun shining in full strength. When I saw him, I fell at his feet as though dead.[122]

Later we encounter Jesus again:

Then I saw heaven opened, and behold, a white horse! The one sitting on it is called Faithful and True, and in righteousness he judges and makes war. His eyes are like a flame of fire, and on his head are many diadems, and he has a name written that no one knows but himself. He is clothed in a robe dipped in blood, and the name by which he is called is The Word of God. And the armies of heaven,

---

[121] Revelation 1:1

[122] Revelation 1:13-17

arrayed in fine linen, white and pure, were following him on white horses. From his mouth comes a sharp sword with which to strike down the nations, and he will rule them with a rod of iron. He will tread the winepress of the fury of the wrath of God the Almighty. On his robe and on his thigh he has a name written, King of kings and Lord of lords.[123]

John sees these visions of Jesus, not as a baby in a manger, nor as a broken man on a cross, but as the risen and ascended and victorious Son of God who is King of kings and Lord of lords. Jesus is Lord was the seminal confession of the early church and it is the theme which holds this book together. If we read Revelation and come away with a different conclusion or an alternative overarching theme, then we may need to go back and read it again.

Whenever I talk about the fact that Jesus is Lord, I get the feeling that some people think it is a distant heavenly rule and one day when Jesus returns then his rule will have earthly implications. But this is to misunderstand what we mean when we say, '*Jesus is Lord.*'

Jesus is not 'Lord-elect' as though he is still to be given the position and title at some point in the future. Jesus is Lord here and now. He is presently Earth's true Lord, true Governor, true Ruler and not a future reality which we await.

Furthermore he is not only the Lord of Christians as though we make him Lord by inviting him into our hearts. He is the Lord of Heaven and Earth who has all authority, and it is only Christians who have yet realised it and chosen to live as though it is true. It is we who bear witness with our words and our lives to God's alternative arrangement of the present world under his King.

It should be clear the message of Jesus isn't just a private spirituality which aims to make us moral people. It is a Kingdom which confronts the kingdoms of the world and their way of doing and being and ultimately smashes them to

[123] Revelation 19:11-16

pieces.[124] It is a message which is politically subversive, economically revolutionary, and socially transformative.[125] And this Kingdom is here, now. This is precisely what is happening in the book of Revelation as Jesus looms large, effects his judgments for his people against Jerusalem, Rome, and ultimately the satan himself.

This is a book which reveals Jesus for the sake of his people who were oppressed and persecuted, so that they might take courage in the fact that the story doesn't end with evil and Empire triumphing (though it may have seemed to be the case right then), but with Jesus and his people victorious.

Perhaps then an alternative title for Revelation could be:

Jesus wins.

[124] Recall the vision from Daniel 2.

[125] Thanks to Alexander Venter for this beautiful phrase.

CHAPTER EIGHTEEN

4 x 7 = Judgment

If the book of Revelation centres on the revelation of Jesus, then it is specifically the judgments of Jesus which constitute the bulk of this book. We have become accustomed to the idea of judgment as being purely negative: the just condemnation of the wicked. However, when God judges it is an expression of his love. Judgment is always with a view to set things right and to restore, not just an act to condemn the guilty. When God judges the earth, the earth and all in it rejoice for it means the end of oppression, injustice, violence, and evil:

Let the heavens be glad, and let the earth rejoice;
let the sea roar, and all that fills it;
let the field exult, and everything in it!
Then shall all the trees of the forest sing for joy
before the Lord, for he comes,
for he comes to judge the earth.[126]

This is what we should keep in mind when we read about God's judgments: they are with a view to setting things right, and the removal of all that stands in the way of that end.

The most obvious judgments in the book of Revelation are the 4 sets of 7 judgments which come in the form of 7 seals, 7 trumpets, 7 thunders, and 7 bowls. These 4 sets of 7 judgments have been used by many teachers to describe how God is going to judge the world in the days to come, taking the imagery quite literally at some points as we will see.

[126] Psalm 96:11-13

But I don't believe that is what we are to take away from these judgments. It is my belief that these are judgments which have already taken place, directed towards Jerusalem and the Temple, fulfilled in 70 A.D. Allow me to show you how I've arrived at that conclusion.

In order to do that I need to go back.

Way back.

In the book of Leviticus, the people of Israel are given the specifics of God's Law and the terms of the covenant. It says if they would obey and faithfully follow God they would be blessed.[127] They would dwell securely, no one would terrorise them, God would dwell with them, their fields would be blessed, no harmful beasts would dwell in their land, and war would not run through their land. Later, Moses summarised this in Deuteronomy 28 saying they would be blessed going in, blessed going out. Their baskets blessed, their wombs blessed, their kneading bowls blessed, and their animals blessed. They would be blessed in the city and blessed in the field. They would be overtaken by blessing.

But if they chose to disobey God and turn away from him, then God would judge them:

But if you will not listen to me and will not do all these commandments … but break my covenant, then I will do this to you: … I will discipline you again sevenfold for your sins … Then if you walk contrary to me and will not listen to me, I will continue striking you, sevenfold for your sins. … And if by this discipline you are not turned to me but walk contrary to me, then I also will walk contrary to you, and I myself will strike you sevenfold for your sins. … But if in spite of this you will not listen to me, but walk contrary to me, then I will walk contrary to you in fury, and I myself will discipline you sevenfold for your sins. You shall eat the flesh of your sons, and you

[127] See Leviticus 26

shall eat the flesh of your daughters. And I will destroy your high places and cut down your incense altars and cast your dead bodies upon the dead bodies of your idols, and my soul will abhor you. And I will lay your cities waste and will make your sanctuaries desolate, and I will not smell your pleasing aromas. And I myself will devastate the land, so that your enemies who settle in it shall be appalled at it. And I will scatter you among the nations, and I will unsheathe the sword after you, and your land shall be a desolation, and your cities shall be a waste.[128]

Here we have God's covenant promise of judgment against his people should they again and again turn away from Him.

Notice that it is 4 sets of 7 fold judgment.

This is what I believe Jesus was saying to the Jewish leaders in Matthew 23 when he announced all the righteous blood of Abel to Zachariah would come upon that generation. It was a covenantal judgment which was unique and never to be repeated. No other generation would ever have to face that judgment again.

It is not coincidental that Revelation records 4 sets of 7 judgments because this is God's covenant judgment of Jerusalem and the Temple. Based on the dating of Revelation, my understanding of Matthew 24, and God's covenant with Israel, I see the 4 x 7 judgment as unfolding during the fall of Jerusalem in 70 A.D.

I will now briefly run through the sets of judgments to show how they overlap with historical data during this time. (Keep in mind what I said previously: these 4 sets of 7 judgments do not necessarily happen sequentially. Rather, they are sequential recounting of a single narrative which overlap and run concurrently.)

[128] Leviticus 26:14-33

7 SEALS

(Revelation 6:1 - 8:1)

Let's begin with the 7 seals. John sees a vision of God the Father holding a scroll with 7 seals on it. No one is found worthy to open the scroll until Jesus steps forward. He alone is worthy to take the scroll and open the seals:

And he went and took the scroll from the right hand of him who was seated on the throne. And when he had taken the scroll, the four living creatures and the twenty-four elders fell down before the Lamb, each holding a harp, and golden bowls full of incense, which are the prayers of the saints. And they sang a new song, saying, "Worthy are you to take the scroll and to open its seals, for you were slain, and by your blood you ransomed people for God from every tribe and language and people and nation, and you have made them a kingdom and priests to our God, and they shall reign on the earth."[129]

Jesus takes the scroll and begins to open it, opening one seal at a time. With the opening of each seal a judgment is released on the Earth. The first 4 seals are what have come to be known as, 'the 4 horsemen of the apocalypse.'[130] I believe each of these, and the remaining 3 seals, find a parallel in the judgment Jesus spoke about in Matthew 24 (which we covered earlier in the book). For the sake of brevity and clarity I will express this parallel in a table format:

7 SEALS	PARALLEL
Horseman #1: Conquest (Revelation 6:2)	Nation against nation, kingdom against kingdom (Matthew 24:7)
Horseman #2: War (Revelation 6:3)	Wars and rumours of wars (Matthew 24:6)
Horseman #3: Famine (Revelation 6:5)	Famines (Matthew 24:7)
Horseman #4: Death (Revelation 6:7)	Natural consequences of the above.

[129] Revelation 5:7-10

[130] Which is an awesome name for a punk rock band.

Martyrs under the altar (Revelation 6:9)	Tribulation and persecution (Matthew 24:9)
Earthquake, Sun and Moon darkened, stars fall, people crying out in fear (Revelation 6:12)	Earthquakes, Sun and Moon darkened, stars falling, people mourning (Matthew 24:7 & 29)
Silence (Revelation 8:1)	Devastation after the fall of Jerusalem

7 TRUMPETS

(Revelation 8:2 - 9:21)

Following the 7 seals are the 7 trumpets.

7 TRUMPETS	PARALLEL
Hail and fire destroy a third of the earth (Revelation 8:7)	Josephus notes how the Romans turned the region around Jerusalem into a desert during the time of the siege.
Great mountain thrown into the sea (Revelation 8:8)	Jerusalem is the mountain of God which Jesus had hinted at being thrown into the sea.
Star called Wormwood (Revelation 8:10)	"[I]n the OT wormwood is used of God's punishment of the wicked, including their death," (see for example Jeremiah 9:15; 23:15 and Lamentations 3:15)
Sun, Moon, and stars struck (Revelation 8:12)	In Scripture, cosmic language is used as a metaphor for authorities and rulers.
Plague of locusts tormenting the land for 5 months (Revelation 9:3)	This is imagery hinting back to the plagues of Egypt, only this time is it Israel on the receiving end. This speaks of the Roman siege which lasted 5 months, whose armies swarmed like locusts devouring everything in sight.

Release of four angels at the Euphrates River with 200 million mounted troops (Revelation 9:13)	Josephus writes how Titus drew on 3000 soldiers stationed at the Euphrates River to join his assault on Jerusalem.
Jesus is victorious, claims back the kingdom of the world, and the Ark of the Covenant is seen in Heaven (Revelation 11:15)	Jesus is Lord of Earth and Heaven, and the inauguration of a New Covenant.

7 THUNDERS

(Revelation 10:1-4)

Between the 6th and 7th trumpet there is another set of judgments which come in the form of thunder:

And when the seven thunders had sounded, I was about to write, but I heard a voice from heaven saying, "Seal up what the seven thunders have said, and do not write it down."[131]

As per the angel's instructions to John he did not record what the 7 thunders represent. However, John is immediately given a scroll to eat which is sweet in his mouth but bitter in his stomach. A Jew, or indeed anyone who knows their Old Testament scriptures, would immediately recall Ezekiel (a prophet long before John) who was also given a scroll to eat which was sweet in his mouth. He was then commanded by God to prophesy against the house of Israel and to physically portray a siege of Jerusalem as a sign of it's judgment and fall.[132] Again I conclude that these 7 fold judgments of thunder seem to be directed towards the house of Israel, as the previous seals and trumpets.

---

[131] Revelation 10:4

[132] Ezekiel 3 & 4

7 BOWLS

(Revelation 16:1-21)

The final set of judgments are the 7 bowls. These judgments seem to be reminiscent of the plagues in Egypt at the time of the Exodus, only this time, Jerusalem is the recipient of the plagues. God always moves history forward redemptively, and whenever people (or a nation) keeps others from moving forward, God will act to liberate and judge — whether it be Egyptians (as in Exodus) or Jews (as in Matthew 24 and much of the book of Revelation).

7 BOWLS	PARALLEL
Bowl #1: Painful sores comes on those who receive the mark of the beast (i.e. capitulate to Caesar worship).	Plague #6: Boils
Bowl #2: Sea turned to blood	Plague #1: Water, rivers, canals, ponds turned to blood
Bowl #3: Rivers turned to blood	Plague #1: Water, rivers, canals, ponds turned to blood
Bowl #4: Sun scorching people	No identifiable parallel
Bowl #5: Bowl poured out upon the throne of the beast and its kingdom is plunged into darkness.	Plague #9: Darkness
Bowl #6: Euphrates dries up to prepare the way for an army, unclean spirits like frogs.	Plague #2: Frogs
Bowl #7: Earthquake, great city split into 3 parts, plague of hailstones.	Plague #7: Hail

These are the 4 sets of 7 fold judgment recorded in the book of Revelation. I believe these were targeted at Jerusalem and the Temple, and ended with Jerusalem's destruction. Both the historical information we have seems to correspond with the text, as well as the connection with the covenantal judgment of God as laid out in Leviticus 26.

Putting the pieces together leads me to conclude that these judgments in Revelation are not about a future Armageddon, but are referring to what took place in the first century soon after John's writing. We therefore do not need to be afraid of some terrifying set of judgments which God will pour out on the whole earth as is taught by many futurist teachers.[133]

This deals with the most prominent set of judgments we encounter in the book of Revelation, but there are a couple of other places where judgment takes place which we will deal with in the next chapters.

---

[133] Futurist teachers are those who teach that the prophecies of Jesus in Matthew 24 and most of the visions contained in the book of Revelation are still to be fulfilled in the future.

CHAPTER NINETEEN

2 Witnesses

Then I was given a measuring rod like a staff, and I was told, "Rise and measure the temple of God and the altar and those who worship there, but do not measure the court outside the temple; leave that out, for it is given over to the nations, and they will trample the holy city for forty-two months. And I will grant authority to my two witnesses, and they will prophesy for 1,260 days, clothed in sackcloth."[134]

In this chapter we will talk briefly about the mystery of the 2 witnesses. But before we do that there is a subject raised by this text which must be addressed: the Temple.

John here is told to measure the Temple of God and those who worship there. The Temple (Herod's Temple in the first century — the Temple Jesus ministered in) was destroyed in 70 A.D. So either this text was written before then and refers to Herod's Temple, or it was written later and was written about some time in the future when the destroyed Temple would be rebuilt. In the Appendix, I make the case that Revelation was written before 70 A.D.[135] and therefore before the Temple was destroyed. I therefore believe that the Temple it refers to is Herod's Temple.

Those who teach a future fulfilment of these texts ('futurists') say that the Temple must be rebuilt in Jerusalem in order for these prophecies to be fulfilled. Let us think carefully about this because we are discussing more than just Middle Eastern politics — we are getting to the heart of God's purposes and his means

---

[134] Revelation 11:1-3

[135] See Appendix: When was the book of Revelation written?

of salvation. Here is an important line of questioning which will highlight exactly what I mean:

How are people reconciled to God?

Through a Temple and a sacrificial system?

Through an Old Covenant involving blood and priests?

Or through Jesus who is both the High Priest and the Lamb who was the Final Sacrifice once and for all?

Does God have one plan for Gentiles and a different plan for Jews? (Gentiles saved and reconciled through Jesus whilst Jews through Temple and sacrifice).

Why would God want the Temple rebuilt at all?

If Jesus re-constituted the people of God around himself, and declared himself to be the new Temple[136] along with his followers,[137] why would God resurrect the old Temple and its system?

Furthermore, sometimes the rebuilding of the Temple is connected with the prophecies of Jesus returning to take his place on David's throne which would require a rebuilding of the Temple. No Temple, no Davidic Ruler. However, Peter says in his sermon in Acts 2 (as does Paul in Acts 13) that Jesus is already seated on the throne of David by virtue of his resurrection and ascension. These 2 make it abundantly clear: we are not waiting for a future moment when Jesus will return to sit on David's throne, as he already occupies that position.

I conclude from the timing of the authorship of Revelation, the fulfilment of the Davidic prophecies, as well as the purposes and means of God in salvation, that

---

[136] John 2:18-22

[137] 1 Corinthians 3:16-17, 6:19

this text in Revelation 11 isn't speaking of a future Temple, but about Herod's 1st century Temple. We are not therefore waiting for a future Temple to be built in Jerusalem on the site of the old one as a sign of the fulfilment of Biblical prophecy.[138]

Now to the 2 witnesses.

Futurist teachers envision 2 men walking through the streets of Jerusalem during part of a 7 year tribulation. But I believe it is more plausible to consider the alternative.

It says that they prophesy for 1260 days which is equal to 3 1/2 years, or 42 months — the same amount of time spoken about just a verse before during which time the nations would trample the Holy City. This connection leads me to believe they were prophesying during the period of the siege of Jerusalem when we could say the armies of Rome (made up of multiple different nations) surrounded the city for 3 1/2 years.[139] They were clothed in sackcloth which meant they were mourning and therefore had a tragic message to bring. Under Mosaic Law, at least 2 witnesses were required before anyone could be declared guilty and sentenced. John continues:

These are the two olive trees and the two lampstands that stand before the Lord of the earth. And if anyone would harm them, fire pours from their mouth and consumes their foes. If anyone would harm them, this is how he is doomed to be killed. They have the power to shut the sky, that no rain may fall during the days of

---

[138] Does this mean there will never be another Temple? Maybe. Maybe not. But I am certain that it will not be because God is resurrecting an Old Covenant sacrificial system, and it will not be a 'marker' of the End Times. Rather if this does happen it will be nothing more than the misplaced ambition of people. Jesus is, and always will be, God's Temple and his final and ultimate sacrifice.

[139] Vespasian was commissioned by Nero in February of A.D. 67, and the city fell in August under the command of Titus (Vespasian's son) in August of A.D. 70. (As an aside, when dealing with apocalyptic literature such as Revelation, it is difficult to know when to take numbers literally and when to understand them in a more symbolic way. In this instance, it seems to me to match the historical record we have which is why I have favoured a literal interpretation of that time.)

their prophesying, and they have power over the waters to turn them into blood and to strike the earth with every kind of plague, as often as they desire.[140]

The first question we ask must be: *Are the two witnesses actual people?*

If so much of Revelation is apocalyptic in nature, and therefore wildly metaphorical, why should we necessarily take it literally at this point? It may very well be referring to two actual people, but we should remain open to the possibility that these are not two individuals.

Next, there is a lot of detail here that we must pay attention to.

When you hear about someone who has the authority to shut the skies so that no rain falls, who comes to mind?

If you know the Old Testament scriptures, Elijah should ring a bell.[141]

Next, who was the Old Testament figure who turned water into blood and struck the earth with every kind of plague?

Moses fits the profile.[142]

It was both Elijah and Moses who saw fire come down from Heaven.[143]

If we are to go by the signs alone, Moses and Elijah are strong contenders for the positions.

When Jesus was on Mount Tabor, he was together with three of his disciples when he was transfigured before them. Alongside Jesus two people appeared

[140] Revelation 11:4-6

[141] 1 Kings 17

[142] Exodus 7-10

[143] Elijah in 2 Kings 1 and Moses Exodus 9:23.

with Him: Moses and Elijah. Peter said, "it is good for us to be here, let's build 3 tents for you guys." God then speaks from Heaven: "*This is my Son, my Chosen One; listen to him!*"[144] When the disciples look up, Moses and Elijah are gone. I believe something significant was happening here in that God was saying, you have heard Moses and Elijah as representatives of the Law and the Prophets, but the Law and the Prophets speak of Jesus. So now, this is my Son, listen to Him! He is the point of convergence of all the Scriptures.

Here in Revelation we have two witnesses which sound like Moses and Elijah, and like on Mount Tabor I believe they represent the Law and the Prophets. During the 3 1/2 years of war before the destruction of Jerusalem, the Law and the Prophets 'testified' against the Jews in that they had violated the covenant of God. Therefore the curses and judgment of Deuteronomy 28, Leviticus 26, and the prophetic tradition, quite literally prophesied destruction over them for the entire duration of the war. This is what I believe the 2 witnesses are referring to.

When they have finished their testimony, the beast that rises from the bottomless pit will make war on them and conquer them and kill them, and their dead bodies will lie in the street of the great city that symbolically is called Sodom and Egypt, where their Lord was crucified. For three and a half days some from the peoples and tribes and languages and nations will gaze at their dead bodies and refuse to let them be placed in a tomb, and those who dwell on the earth will rejoice over them and make merry and exchange presents, because these two prophets had been a torment to those who dwell on the earth. But after the three and a half days a breath of life from God entered them, and they stood up on their feet, and great fear fell on those who saw them. Then they heard a loud voice from heaven saying to them, "Come up here!" And they went up to heaven in a cloud, and their enemies watched them. And at that hour there was a great earthquake, and a tenth of the city fell. Seven thousand people were killed in the earthquake, and the rest were terrified and gave glory to the God of heaven.[145]

---

[144] Luke 9:35

[145] Revelation 11:7-13

This vision goes on to say that the two witnesses were killed by the beast and then three days later rose from the dead. What could this mean?

My theory[146] is that the testimony of the Law and the Prophets were put to death by Rome (the beast — we will deal with this in the next chapter) when they finally breached the walls of Jerusalem and laid the city to waste. The early Christians didn't yet have a New Testament and since the Law and the Prophets testified about Jesus, they used the Jewish Scriptures as authoritative and witnessed to Jesus through them. So whilst the Law and the Prophets seemed to fall with Jerusalem and it's Temple ("the great city that symbolically is called Sodom and Egypt"), they found new life through the Church.

The two witnesses are certainly enigmatic figures in the Revelation text and I don't believe we can be too dogmatic one way or the other. However, I think we can remain open to the possibility that they referred to events which took place in history past, rather than to events which lie in our future.

[146] This is one of those tricky pieces of the puzzle of which I am less sure of than I am of other pieces.

CHAPTER TWENTY

The Beasts

And I saw a beast rising out of the sea, with ten horns and seven heads, with ten diadems on its horns and blasphemous names on its heads. And the beast that I saw was like a leopard; its feet were like a bear's, and its mouth was like a lion's mouth. And to it the dragon gave his power and his throne and great authority. One of its heads seemed to have a mortal wound, but its mortal wound was healed, and the whole earth marveled as they followed the beast. And they worshiped the dragon, for he had given his authority to the beast, and they worshiped the beast, saying, "Who is like the beast, and who can fight against it?"[147]

Ahh, the beast. At last we meet. Here we find one of the most well known characters within the pages of this mysterious book. This is a textbook case of apocalyptic language at work, which means we aren't meant to read it literally and expect a beast with 7 heads and 10 horns arising out of the sea (now that is good news!). So what then are we to expect? First, we can take a lesson from Daniel.

Daniel is a book which Jesus, John and others would have been familiar with when it came to the genre of writing known as apocalyptic. According to Daniel 7, a beast can represent either a king or a kingdom and a horn can represent a king.[148] We know this interpretation is correct because this same beast appears just four chapters later, in Revelation 17, with further explanation:

---

[147] Revelation 13:1-4

[148] Daniel 7:17, 23-24

But the angel said to me ... "I will tell you the mystery ... of the beast with seven heads and ten horns ... the seven heads are seven mountains on which the woman is seated; they are also seven kings, five of whom have fallen, one is; the other has not yet come, and when he does come he must remain only a little while. ... And the ten horns that you saw are ten kings who have not yet received royal power, but they are to receive authority as kings for one hour, together with the beast.[149]

So the information we have is this: the beast represents seven mountains.

One possible interpretation is that this represents Rome since it is a city with it's famed seven mountains.[150] Based on what we already know about the dating of this book, it is a strong possibility that the beast represents Rome and the Roman Empire.

We are also told the seven heads represent seven kings, five of which have fallen, one is, and one is still to come but only for a short while.

There is a time in the first century which matches this exact timeline of kings. Part of the reason why I hold to an earlier dating of the writing of the book of Revelation (sometime in the early 60's[151]), is because history lines up quite neatly with this text. 5 kings (or horns) that "*have fallen*" are the first five Caesars: Julius (49 BC — 44 B.C.), Augustus (27 B.C. – 14 A.D.), Tiberius (14–37 A.D.), Caligula (37–41 A.D.), Claudius (41–54 A.D.). The 6th king that "*is*" was Caesar Nero (who ruled between 54–68 A.D.), and the 1 which remains "*only a little while*" was Caesar Galba who reigned for 7 months (68–69 A.D.).

My conclusion is that the beast spoken about in Revelation represented the Roman Empire which was at that time being ruled by Caesar Nero.

---

149 Revelation 17:7-12

150 There was even a movie in the 1950's by the name Seven Hills of Rome.

151 See Appendix: When was the book of Revelation written?

The mortal head wound which had been healed referred to the upheaval which followed Nero's sudden suicide. His death marked the end of the Julio-Claudian line of emperors which had begun with Julius Caesar. Following Nero's death, the Roman Empire had 4 emperors in a single year. It was a time when it looked as though Rome would crumble under the weight of infighting and civil war — that Rome itself might fall. Vespasian however, managed to bring things under control and restored peace, establishing a new line of the Flavian dynasty, reviving the Empire.

During these years, the Roman Empire was a powerful force on the earth with massive, trained, disciplined armies led by generals skilled in strategy. In that day it could very easily be said, "*Who is like the beast? And who can fight against it?*"[152] F.W. Farrar, a well respected Anglican and scholar of the late 19th century said:

Every Jewish reader, of course, saw that the Beast was a symbol of Nero. ... All the earliest Christian writers on the Apocalypse, from Irenaeus down to Victorinus of Pettau and Commodian in the fourth, and Andreas in the Fifth, and St. Beatus in the eighth century, connect Nero, or some Roman Emperor, with the Apocalyptic Beast.

Another piece of history which lines up with this conclusion can be found in the next verses:

And the beast was given a mouth uttering haughty and blasphemous words, and it was allowed to exercise authority for forty-two months. ... Also it was allowed to make war on the saints and to conquer them. ... Here is a call for the endurance and faith of the saints.[153]

---

[152] Revelation 13:4

[153] Revelation 13:5-10

In 64 A.D., a fire broke out in Rome destroying a third of the city. Some believed Nero himself had set the fire but Nero blamed the Christians, which began a period of intense persecution which continued under Nero until his death 3 1/2 years later which is 42 months.

The history certainly seems to line up quite neatly. The beast spoken about in Revelation 13 is not a future empire or world ruler, but rather is a symbol for the Roman Empire and of Nero in particular as it's head at that point in history.

CHAPTER TWENTY-ONE

Mark of the Beast

After seeing a vision of a dragon and a beast, John sees a second beast. The first beast arose out of the sea while this second beast arises out of the land and makes people worship the first beast.

I believe this first beast is seen as arising from across the sea because Rome is geographically across the sea from Israel. This second beast arises from the land because it represents a local Roman official who enforces allegiance and worship of Caesar who was based in Rome. It says of this second beast:

Also it causes all, both small and great, both rich and poor, both free and slave, to be marked on the right hand or the forehead, so that no one can buy or sell unless he has the mark, that is, the name of the beast or the number of its name. This calls for wisdom: let the one who has understanding calculate the number of the beast, for it is the number of a man, and his number is 666.[154]

Here we encounter the infamous 'mark of the beast'. Many believe the mark of the beast is a future technology which will be implanted under our skin, and if you receive it you will go to hell. Personally, I find that very hard to believe.

Firstly, this interpretation doesn't do justice to how the first century readers understood it.

These visions in Revelation were supposed to encourage the churches to remain faithful to Jesus even whilst being persecuted by the Jews and the Empire. Why

[154] Revelation 13:16-18

then would it have been important for the first century church to be told about a chip 2,000 years into the future?

If we are to have an understanding of the mark of the beast, we must first understand the context of this text is worship. If we have understood things correctly up till now, the local official(s) are enforcing Caesar worship and compelling people to worship Nero as the head of the Roman Empire. If you worship Nero or his image, you receive a mark as a sign of your worship.[155]

In many of the marketplaces of that time, there was an altar where you would make an offering to Caesar as a sign of your allegiance to the Empire and worship of the Emperor and then use some of the ash to mark your head or hand as a symbol of that offering. Only then could you go into the marketplace to buy and sell.

As a Christian you were faced with a choice: capitulate to Caesar and the Empire and everything will be all right — except your integrity as one of the followers of Jesus. Resist, and you will face the sword of Caesar.

For me, this offers the best interpretation of the mark of the beast. It was an issue of worship and devotion.

Let me say this though: if in the future there is a tattoo, or implanted chip, or some marking which will be used as a symbol of my worship and allegiance to anyone or anything other than Jesus, then count me out. I only hope that I would have the courage and faith to resist it as those early believers did.

However, if you are going to buy into the latest conspiracies about the mark of the beast being some new microchip implanted into a person's body which stores their medical information (as one amongst many biological and scientific

[155] The Imperial Cult is a well known historical phenomenon. The Caesars were not only political figures to be obeyed and followed, they were religious figures to be worshipped. Check out N.T. Wright's article Paul and Caesar: A New Reading of Romans at http://ntwrightpage.com/2016/07/12/paul-and-caesar-a-new-reading-of-romans/ (accessed 27 March 2017)

ideas) and then say this is the mark of the beast, then please make the case for me why someone would go to hell for that?

What then can we say about 666?

Many people throughout history have tried to figure out who the person is who's name calculates to 666. Truth be told, you can make almost anyone's name add up to 666 if you try hard enough. Far more plausible is the gematria of Caesar Nero. The gematria was a system existing in the first century which assigned numbers to letters. The Hebrew spelling of Caesar Nero was NRWN QSR (pronounced Neron Kesar), which calculates to 666 in the following way:

Nrwn Qsr
Q=100
S=60
R=200
N=50
R=200
W=6
N=50
Total = 666

Of course, the names of many other people will calculate to 666, but so many pieces of the puzzle fit together with this interpretation and they all point to Nero and the Roman Empire. It would be tough to twist the straightforward evidence we have, based on the dating of the book and the facts of history, and point it in another direction.

Simply put then, do not be afraid.

CHAPTER TWENTY-TWO

Antichrist

With the question of the beast and the mark of the beast comes the question of the antichrist.

Who is the antichrist?

Many people say the beast and the antichrist are one and the same. But did you know the book of Revelation never mentions the antichrist. Not once. The only place in the Bible you will find the antichrist mentioned is in 1 and 2 John which are two letters written by John the disciple of Jesus.

How do people connect the antichrist in John with the beast in Revelation?

I don't know.

What I do know is people have connected dots which are not connected and have created this powerful, terrifying, antichrist figure. But I don't believe this is being faithful with the texts. I believe the beast in Revelation is different to the antichrist, and I'm about to show you why.

Starting with the letters of 1 and 2 John, what you find is that the antichrist is not one specific person but rather a spirit or a demonic influence over people's lives:

Children, it is the last hour, and as you have heard that antichrist is coming, so now many antichrists have come. … Who is the liar but he who denies that Jesus is the Christ? This is the antichrist, he who denies the Father and the Son. …every spirit that confesses that Jesus Christ has come in the flesh is from God, and every spirit that does not confess Jesus is not from God. This is the spirit of the antichrist, which you heard was coming and now is in the world already. … For many deceivers have gone out into the world, those who do not confess the coming of Jesus Christ in the flesh. Such a one is the deceiver and the antichrist.[156]

Believe it or not but we have just read every single text on the antichrist **in the whole Bible**.

It seems like someone is making a whole lot out of very little.

Nevertheless, what are the criteria which identify the antichrist? I mean, if you were applying for the job of antichrist, what would you need on your resumé?

Do you have to be a powerful world leader?

Do you have to be the Pope of the Catholic Church?

Do you have to be the one who could restore peace to the Middle East?

Do you have to threaten to change dates on a calendar?[157]

Nope.

None of the above.

According to John, all you have to do is **deny that Jesus has come in the flesh.**

That's it. That's all you have to do to become the antichrist.[158]

---

[156] 1 John 2:18,22; 4:2-3 & 2 John 1:7

[157] See Daniel 7:25

[158] Simple huh? One wonders why more people haven't applied for the job…

John was writing at a time when Gnosticism was growing in popularity and being assimilated by the early churches into their beliefs. Gnostics essentially taught that matter is evil and spirit is good. They argued that Jesus couldn't have come in the flesh because he would then have partaken of that which is physical and therefore evil and unclean. John was warning the church against such a doctrine, because it undermined the very substance of our salvation and faith. Such a spirit was "anti-Christ".

Another connection that is often made with the beast and the antichrist is the 'man of lawlessness' from the second letter of Paul to the Thessalonians:

Now concerning the coming of our Lord Jesus Christ and our being gathered together to him, we ask you, brothers, not to be quickly shaken in mind or alarmed, either by a spirit or a spoken word, or a letter seeming to be from us, to the effect that the day of the Lord has come. Let no one deceive you in any way. For that day will not come, unless the rebellion comes first, and the man of lawlessness is revealed, the son of destruction, who opposes and exalts himself against every so-called god or object of worship, so that he takes his seat in the temple of God, proclaiming himself to be God. Do you not remember that when I was still with you I told you these things? And you know what is restraining him now so that he may be revealed in his time. For the mystery of lawlessness is already at work. Only he who now restrains it will do so until he is out of the way. And then the lawless one will be revealed, whom the Lord Jesus will kill with the breath of his mouth and bring to nothing by the appearance of his coming.[159]

To what was Paul referring when he spoke about "*the day of the Lord*"? Was he referring to the end of history? Or was he referring to an event within history itself? I favour the latter interpretation. Tom Wright:

If 'the day of the Lord' meant 'the end of the world', the Thessalonians would not need to be informed of such an event by letter! The Old Testament prophets used

[159] 2 Thessalonians 2:1-8

'the day of the Lord' to refer to catastrophes that befell Jerusalem within continuing history.[160]

Who then could this "*man of lawlessness*" be?

Is he some future individual?

If that was the case then the Temple in Jerusalem would need to be rebuilt for the fulfilment of this text. However, as you already know, I don't believe that the future rebuilding of the Temple is part of God's plan since he has already redefined the Temple in Jesus and the Body of the Christ — the Church.

So I favour an interpretation which locates this in the days before the destruction of Herod's Temple (i.e. before 70 A.D.). After all, Paul did say to his readers in the first century, "*you know what is restraining him now.*"[161] If he was some future figure, Paul could never have said, "hey, ***you guys know him***."

In my opinion there are two possible contenders for the title of the "*man of lawlessness*". But before we speak of them, it will help us to first speak of the one who "*restrains*" him.

In my opinion the clearest candidate for this title is Ananus who was the High Priest in Jerusalem at that time. Josephus described him in this way:

He was on other accounts also a venerable, and a very just man; and besides the grandeur of that nobility, and dignity, and honor of which he was possessed, he had been a lover of a kind of parity, even with regard to the meanest of the people; he was a prodigious lover of liberty, and an admirer of a democracy in government; and did ever prefer the public welfare before his own advantage, and preferred

160 Tom Wright, *Paul for Everyone: Galatians and Thessalonians*, pg. 147

161 vs. 6

peace above all things; for he was thoroughly sensible that the Romans were not to be conquered.[162]

He was a man who knew the Romans could not be conquered and that fighting them would only lead to their own demise. He was a man committed to peace and democracy but was murdered in a bloody attack from within the city which set the city of Jerusalem on a different course — towards destruction. Josephus recognised this as a turning point in the fate of the city:

I should not mistake if I said that the death of Ananus was the beginning of the destruction of the city, and that from this very day may be dated the overthrow of her wall, and the ruin of her affairs, whereon they saw their high priest, and the procurer of their preservation, slain in the midst of their city.[163]

Ananus is, in my opinion, the clearest candidate for the one who restrains the man of lawlessness.

The question remains then: who is this man of lawlessness?

As I said, there are two possible contenders for the title.

The first is a man named John Levi (or John of Gishala). According to Josephus he was an intelligent, conniving man, who weaseled his way into the inner circle of the religious leaders in Jerusalem, gaining their trust so that he might take control of the city. Josephus said, "*he cultivated the greatest friendship possible with Ananus, and with the chief of the people ... so far did they believe him, they they sent him as their ambassador into the temple.*"[164] John's persuasiveness afforded him a position which undoubtedly contributed to the destruction of the city of Jerusalem. Josephus wrote:

---

[162] Josephus, *Wars of the Jews*, Book 4, Chapter 5, Paragraph 2

[163] Ibid.

[164] Ibid., Chapter 3, Paragraph 13

These harangues of John's corrupted a great part of the young men, and puffed them up for the war; but as to the more prudent part, and those in years, there was not a man of them but foresaw what was coming, and made lamentation on that account, as if the city was already undone.[165]

After the death of Ananus, Josephus wrote how it became obvious to the zealots around John that he was "*setting up a monarchy.*"[166] He was essentially setting himself up in a place of authority from within the Temple. There is much resonance here with Paul's words in Thessalonians.

The other contender for this title is Simon son of Giora, "*not so cunning indeed as John [of Gisehala], who had already seized upon the city, but superior in strength of body and courage.*"[167] He had been driven from the Acrabattene toparchy by Ananus, and upon learning of Ananus' death, he sprung to action, retaking it and causing much death and destruction in the surrounding region. He found himself outside the walls of Jerusalem fighting those inside on a number of occasions, before being brought into the city in an attempt to rid those inside of John of Gishala and the zealots. They welcomed him, "*as their savior and preserver; but when he was come in, with his army, he took care to secure his own authority ... And thus did Simon get possession of Jerusalem, in the third year of the war.*"[168]

Whichever of these two it was, it is clear that both were catalysed into action through the death of Ananus who had up until this point restrained the evil perpetrated by both of these leaders. I find these three historical figures offer a possible explanation for the fulfilment of Paul's words, rather than some future "*man of lawlessness*" who will establish himself in a rebuilt Temple in Jerusalem.

---

[165] Ibid., Paragraph 3

[166] Ibid. Chapter 7, Paragraph 1

[167] Ibid. Chapter 9, Paragraph 3

[168] Ibid., Paragraph 11-12

My conclusion then is that the beast from Revelation, the antichrist from 1 and 2 John, and the man of lawlessness from 2 Thessalonians are not one and the same. They are not referring to a single powerful world leader who will appear at some point in our future, but rather to three very different entities more contemporary to their own time.

CHAPTER TWENTY-THREE

The Whore of Babylon

I feel for the Pope.

He gets labelled as so many Biblical names. And none of them good ones.

Antichrist.

Beast.

Purveyor of funny hats.

Ok, I made that last one up.

Here's another one:

Whore of Babylon.

That particular title comes from this text:

Then one of the seven angels who had the seven bowls came and said to me, "Come, I will show you the judgment of the great prostitute who is seated on many waters, with whom the kings of the earth have committed sexual immorality, and with the wine of whose sexual immorality the dwellers on earth have become drunk." And he carried me away in the Spirit into a wilderness, and I saw a woman sitting on a scarlet beast that was full of blasphemous names, and it had seven heads and ten horns. The woman was arrayed in purple and scarlet, and adorned with gold and jewels and pearls, holding in her hand a golden cup full of abominations and the impurities of her sexual immorality. And on her forehead was written a name of mystery: "Babylon the great, mother of prostitutes and of earth's abominations." And I saw the woman, drunk with the blood of the saints, the blood of the martyrs of Jesus. … And the woman that you saw is the great city that has dominion over the kings of the earth.[169]

John sees a vision of a scarlet beast with seven heads and ten horns and riding on this beast he sees a woman dressed in purple and scarlet, adorned with gold, jewels, and pearls, holding a cup of abominations.

And this is supposed to be the Pope.

Really?

This 'woman' has affectionately come to be called the Whore of Babylon.[170]

Notice that John sees this woman in two distinct visions here.

First, he sees her seated on "many waters." Then, John is taken away in the Spirit into a wilderness where he sees her again, this time seated on "a scarlet beast."

What's going on here?

John gives us clues to figuring this question out.

First, John says: "*The woman … is the great city that has dominion over the kings of the earth.*" If you have come this far (and you didn't skip the previous chapters), bells should already be ringing. There is undoubtedly some

[169] Revelation 17:1-6,18

[170] Which, again, is another example of a great name for a punk band.

connection to Rome as the seat of the Roman Empire.[171]

Second, John says, "*The waters that you saw, where the prostitute is seated, are peoples and multitudes and nations and languages.*"[172]

When I put these two pieces together, the conclusion I come to is that she is not the same as the beast (which was the Roman Empire), but rather she represents the satanic power behind all such oppressive, violent, and totalitarian Empires and regimes.[173] She represents the seduction of money, sex, and power (not bad in themselves, but frequently distorted and abused). At that time she happened to be 'riding' the beast of the Roman Empire, but in actual fact she has throughout history saddled herself upon many different empires and regimes. In fact, she rides upon any who would prostitute themselves to her seductive power. I believe Paul referred to this same woman in his letters as the "principalities and powers"[174] — as the power behind the powers.

The truth is, even today we live under an empire. It may not have a face or a figurehead, but it's symbols are everywhere. It is an empire drawing us into it's dominant story and narrative which is a distortion of the way of life expressed by

[171] Some link the Whore of Babylon with ancient Jerusalem which was destroyed in 70 A.D. Within the futurist camp there is little consensus. Some have said she represents a reformed Roman Empire, others the Catholic Church, still others Iraq or the United States.

[172] Revelation 17:15

[173] You might have a different interpretation saying she represents Jerusalem. There may be some evidence for this, however, it seems to me from the flow of the book of Revelation that Jerusalem is judged by the 4 x 7 judgment which is concluded in Rev 16. Then at the end of that chapter it says, "*The great city was split into three parts, and the cities of the nations fell, and God remembered Babylon the great, to make her drain the cup of the wine of the fury of his wrath,*" (Rev 16:19). After judging Jerusalem, God turns his attention to Babylon and then in chapter 17 begins with his judgment against her. This view is supported by multiple commentators including Jamieson, Fausset, and Brown Commentary, Expositors Bible Commentary, and Tom Wright's Revelation for Everyone.

[174] See for example Romans 8:38, Ephesians 3:10, 6:12, Colossians 1:16

Jesus.[175] In the Western world, this 'Empire story' has at least three major themes running through it: capitalism, individualism, and consumerism.

Firstly, capitalism. Capitalism is far more than an efficient system of economics. Capitalism has become the way we think about *everything*. It has become a story we believe about ourselves, others, the world, and even God. The story can be summed up quite simply in this way: everything is a commodity.[176]

Creation is a commodity which we can use for the sake of profit.

Sex is no longer sacred, it's a commodity to be traded.

Time is no longer sacred, because productivity is our greatest goal and so we have productivity gurus who can help us squeeze every ounce of profit from these bodies every day and then help us sleep better so we can do it all again tomorrow, better, faster.

Under this narrative it is difficult not to treat people as tools or objects for a task.

Everything has become a commodity with which we can trade without conscience.

Secondly, individualism has shaped us to be independent and self-reliant, where we favour freedom for individuals or for my family ("me and mine") over our collective responsibility to each other. So within the Western culture we have elevated personal freedoms above love for others.

This narrative has given a transactional shape to our relationships with each other. Individualism has become the water we are swimming in, leaving us

[175] If you want to read more on this I highly recommend *Colossians Remixed: Subverting the Empire* by Brian Walsh and Sylvia Keesmaat. It is a bit academic, but worth the effort. Much of my thinking below has been shaped by them.

[176] See Brian Walsh and Sylvia Keesmaat, *Colossians Remixed: Subverting the Empire*, pg. 137-139

oblivious to the idea that there might be an alternative way to be human in the world.[177]

It has shaped the way we think about what it means to be the church: the church is reduced to a group of isolated individuals who attend a meeting once a week (and if we don't feel like coming, or we're not getting anything out of it, then we don't come). We've forgotten that the church is a body collective and we are joined to each other in love, connected to build each other up as each part of the body does it's work.[178]

We only think this way because we've bought into the dominant storyline of our particular empire.

The third dominant theme of our culture is consumerism which can be described as the preoccupation of a society with the accumulation and consumption of goods for oneself. The problem with consuming in this way with self at the centre, is that it becomes a disordered consumption which indulges but never satisfies.[179]

Our society today can be described as those who are held captive by dissatisfaction. After all, isn't that what advertising is? Trillions and trillions of dollars and euros and rands are being spent to make you dissatisfied. As Barry Jones has said, "*Every television commercial is a thirty second 'beatitude,' a story of what the 'blessed life' looks like.*"[180] The blessed life looks like someone who has what they are peddling.

Consumerism hands us a narrative which leads us to accumulate and upgrade, so that those with the most, and the best, are superior, more important,

[177] Thanks to Jana Niehaus for this relational dimension.

[178] Ephesians 4:16

[179] Again, Walsh and Keesmaat, pg. 137-139

[180] Barry D. Jones, *Dwell: Life with God for the World*, location 1543 (Kindle edition)

valuable, and accepted. One wonders the kind of inner fortitude that is required to resist this kind of force exerted by our empire?

Empire, by nature, makes seductive blasphemous and immoral claims and engages in corollary practices that bring disorder to both vertical (people-God) and horizontal (people-people) human relations, promising life but delivering death—both physical and spiritual.[181]

This gives you a glimpse into our particular brand of Empire today. The Whore of Babylon still rides on today in her pride and seductive intent. Only in our day it isn't the Roman Empire, it's a far more subtle and global expression.

The question for us today is the same as the question for the early church: Have we bought into it's story? Are we participants in it's narrative? Do we bear it's marks of allegiance and worship upon our lives? The words of Revelation need to be heard afresh by us today:

Then I heard another voice from heaven saying,
"Come out of her, my people,
lest you take part in her sins,
lest you share in her plagues;
for her sins are heaped high as heaven,
and God has remembered her iniquities.[182]

Like the early church, we too are called to live in a different narrative. As those who are called to be faithful to Jesus who calls us His bride, we are to resist the seductive temptations offered us in the stories of accumulation and consumption without conscience, pleasure without commitment and sacrifice, and violent oppression, abuse, and coercion (the twisted distortions of money, sex, and power).

---

[181] Michael Gorman, Reading Revelation Responsibly, location 1894 (Kindle edition)

[182] Revelation 18:4-5

There is so much that could be said here regarding the practical implications of this.

For example, in the way we work, do we do things because, "*this is just the way things work in this industry*"? Or do we actively rewrite the terms and conditions of the status quo — in the way we remunerate our employees,[183] in the way we care for creation, in the leadership styles we adopt, and in the general practice of a more honest, generous, and redemptive presence in the world?

In the way we spend our money, buy our clothing, and purchase our food, are we making choices which ensure the flourishing of people's lives all along the supply chain? Or through our purchases are we securing their ongoing practical slavery in far away places, working under oppressive conditions, earning a pittance?

These are tough questions to ask and tougher to answer. The thing about empires like ours (which has been influenced in large part by the West) is that they capture our imaginations, leading us to believe *we have no alternative*. But that's just the lie of the empire which wants to keep us serving it's narrative. Hear the call of Jesus again: "*Come out of her, my people, lest you take part in her sins, lest you share in her plagues.*"[184] We as the people of God must find alternatives and then creatively and imaginatively live them out.

There will come a time when the Whore of Babylon will be judged. The kings of the earth, the traders who did business — all those who invested in the system — will all mourn at her downfall.

---

[183] In my home country of South Africa, we have the biggest gap between the materially rich and the materially poor in the world. Part of the reason is the massive disparity between salaries for those at the top of the organisational chart, and those at the bottom. As those who follow Jesus we must actively disrupt this status quo starting with those of us who employ domestic workers at home and then working this principle out all the way up.

[184] Revelation 18:4

Directly after this whore is judged, Revelation 19 paints the picture of the bride of Christ. This woman is not dressed in gold, jewels, purple and scarlet but in fine linen clean and pure — which are the righteous deeds of the saints.

It is as though the whole book has been leading us to this point.

The Church is the one for whom the judgment is given. The judgment against Jerusalem, the beasts, the dragon, and the whore of Babylon, are for the sake of the Church. The faithful saints who have followed Jesus, who endured persecution and martyrdom, are finally vindicated, and those who oppressed, murdered, and exploited them are called to account and judged.

Herein lies the intent of Jesus, of the angel, and of John in the giving and recording of this book. We are to see Jesus who triumphs, who is Lord and King, and we are to see the people of God vindicated and the enemies of God and his people judged.

One can scarcely imagine how these visions would have been received by a church existing in the first century under the intense and violent persecutions enacted by the Jews, the Romans, and Nero in particular. There would have been much rejoicing, much hope, much comfort, and the early church would have received courage and faith to march forward in their mission and purpose to see God's peaceable and just Kingdom come on Earth as it is in Heaven.

CHAPTER TWENTY-FOUR

Red Dragon

The red dragon of Revelation completes the unholy trinity of evil together with the beast and the whore. Fortunately for us, John doesn't leave us guessing as to the identity of this scaly reptilian: it is the satan himself.

We encounter this red dragon early on in Revelation:

And another sign appeared in heaven: behold, a great red dragon, with seven heads and ten horns, and on his heads seven diadems. His tail swept down a third of the stars of heaven and cast them to the earth. ... Now war arose in heaven, Michael and his angels fighting against the dragon. And the dragon and his angels fought back, but he was defeated, and there was no longer any place for them in heaven. And the great dragon was thrown down, that ancient serpent, who is called the devil and Satan, the deceiver of the whole world—he was thrown down to the earth, and his angels were thrown down with him. And I heard a loud voice in heaven, saying, "Now the salvation and the power and the kingdom of our God and the authority of his Christ have come, for the accuser of our brothers has been thrown down, who accuses them day and night before our God."[185]

John sees the red dragon (satan) thrown down to the Earth from Heaven. The timing of this casting down of the devil coincides with the announcement of "*the salvation and the power and the kingdom of our God and the authority of his Christ.*" What event made this declaration possible? The death and resurrection of Jesus. These two events then are connected in that the devil was thrown down to Earth because of the death and resurrection of Jesus.

[185] Revelation 12:3-4, 7-10

Jesus himself connected his death with the casting out of the devil:

"Now is the judgment of this world; now will the ruler of this world be cast out."[186]

Not only was the "*ruler of this world*" cast out, Jesus said he was also judged:

"*[T]he ruler of this world is judged.*"[187]

A few chapters later in Revelation 20, we encounter this red dragon again:

Then I saw an angel coming down from heaven, holding in his hand the key to the bottomless pit and a great chain. And he seized the dragon, that ancient serpent, who is the devil and Satan, and bound him for a thousand years, and threw him into the pit, and shut it and sealed it over him, so that he might not deceive the nations any longer, until the thousand years were ended. After that he must be released for a little while.[188]

This is one of the more difficult passages to interpret.

When did this take place?

Or is it still to take place?

Is it a literal 1,000 years?

I don't think it's worth getting too dogmatic at this point, but personally I believe that what is said here mirrors what was said in chapter 12 (i.e. this doesn't happen later in time, though it appears later in the book) which means that satan is currently bound with the effect that he cannot deceive the nations any longer.

[186] John 12:31

[187] John 16:11

[188] Revelation 20:1-3

You may say this interpretation is out of touch with reality.

"Just look around! Are you telling me satan isn't influencing what is going on in the world!?"

Let me explain.

First, note how in Revelation 12 we are told the devil is the "*deceiver of the whole world.*"[189] Then because Jesus defeats him through the Cross, he is thrown down to the earth. Now, in Revelation 20, he no longer has the ability to deceive the nations. Satan has been stripped of his power and authority. Once he was the ruler of the world, but now he is not. Once he could deceive the whole world since it lay in his hands, now he has been disempowered, disarmed, and dethroned and can no longer do so. He doesn't have the ability and authority he used to because now all authority in Heaven and on Earth belongs to Jesus.

During his earthly ministry Jesus spoke about binding the strong man so that his house might be plundered.[190] I believe he was making reference to the devil being bound so that his kingdom could be plundered. It seems like Jesus believed the reason he could cast out demons was because the strong man (the devil) was bound. Now that the devil is bound, the kingdom of darkness can be plundered, and the Gospel light can break in with liberating truth. This is why it was possible for Jesus to issue his disciples with the command to make disciples of *all nations*.[191]

Framed in this way it doesn't seem implausible that Revelation 20 refers to events which coincide with the events of Jesus in the first century.

---

189 Revelation 12:9

190 Matthew 12:29

191 Matthew 28:18

As to the 'binding' of the satan (verse 2), Jesus declared that he had already accomplished this, which was why he was able to perform exorcisms (Matthew 12.29). The satan was, after all, still able thereafter to work through Judas and others, to accuse Jesus and bring about his death. Perhaps what we are seeing in Revelation 20 is the cosmic version of that story.[192]

So is there still demonic influence or opposition anymore? Of course there is. Somehow Jesus could bind the strongman but still need to drive out demons. He bound the devil but the devil could still influence Judas. The one truth doesn't automatically exclude the other. One theory is that perhaps it is the devil himself who is bound but his demons (the third of the stars we read about in Revelation 12) are still operating, though with greatly reduced effectiveness wherever the Kingdom of God is present.

Again, we shouldn't get too dogmatic on this point. Whatever our view is on this text, I'm sure we will agree that evil is still a presence in our world, but light is more powerful than darkness so there is no contest between God and the devil. We have therefore been authorised in the name of Jesus to plunder the kingdom of darkness through the preaching of the Gospel, the healing of the sick, the casting out of demons, and the raising of the dead. This is possible because Jesus has won absolute victory.

What then about the 1,000 years?

Are we to take it literally?

Well, if we use the Hebrew text (the Old Testament) as a guide, the number 1,000 is used in a couple of places[193] where they are not intended to be taken literally, but are better understood to mean, 'a large amount'.

---

[192] Tom Wright, *Revelation for Everyone*, pg. 180

[193] See Deuteronomy 7:9; Psalm 50:10; 84:10

And when the thousand years are ended, Satan will be released from his prison and will come out to deceive the nations that are at the four corners of the earth, Gog and Magog, to gather them for battle; their number is like the sand of the sea. And they marched up over the broad plain of the earth and surrounded the camp of the saints and the beloved city, but fire came down from heaven and consumed them, and the devil who had deceived them was thrown into the lake of fire and sulfur where the beast and the false prophet were, and they will be tormented day and night forever and ever.[194]

Why is the satan afforded one final opportunity to deceive the nations? I don't know. Whatever it is, I'm sure God has a good reason. The point here however is that the day will come (which I believe still remains in the future) when the dragon himself — the satan and devil — will be thrown into a place of torment forever. The sentence which currently hangs over his head will be carried out with finality. No longer will he be allowed to influence or deceive ever again. Finally God will deal with evil and expel it.

[194] Revelation 20:7-10

CHAPTER TWENTY-FIVE

Millennium

Then I saw thrones, and seated on them were those to whom the authority to judge was committed. Also I saw the souls of those who had been beheaded for the testimony of Jesus and for the word of God, and those who had not worshiped the beast or its image and had not received its mark on their foreheads or their hands. They came to life and reigned with Christ for a thousand years. The rest of the dead did not come to life until the thousand years were ended. This is the first resurrection. Blessed and holy is the one who shares in the first resurrection! Over such the second death has no power, but they will be priests of God and of Christ, and they will reign with him for a thousand years.[195]

This is the text which falls under the heading of 'The Millennium' or 'the Millennial reign of Christ'.

Much is made of 'the Millennium'.

In fact it is the Millennium which defines four main brands of end times teaching (amillenialism, pre-millenial dispensationalism, historical pre-millenialism, post-millenialism).[196] The fact that people define their eschatology (beliefs about the End Times) around the Millennium tells you that this is not a straightforward text to interpret.

Having said that, to me it is strange to make so much of so little.

[195] Revelation 20:4-6

[196] You don't need to know what they are, but just know that the Millennium is important to many people when talking about the end times. See the Appendix for some help understanding these terms.

This is the only place in Scripture where the Millennium is mentioned and yet it has become the hinge on which most people's end times theology turns (whether they realise it or not).

For me, that would be giving it too central a role.

The big point which many make when referring to this Millennium is that it is connected with the reign of Jesus. In other words, Jesus begins to reign when the Millennium begins. A problem I have is that many see the Millennium as still in the future and having not begun yet, and so they see Jesus not yet reigning on Earth. Can you see the flow of logic? I would imagine that pressed on the issue, some futurist teachers might say that Jesus is reigning in Heaven but not on Earth.[197] But I can only guess.

I believe this conclusion is a mistake. And when we take a road which ends up in a strange destination, it is time to retrace our steps and figure out where we made a wrong turn and maybe ask for directions.

The fundamental mistake that is being made here is the assumption that these two subjects are conjoined (i.e. that the Millennium and the rule of Jesus are connected).

In my opinion these concepts have been incorrectly glued together using this text.

Let's ask some questions so you'll see what I mean.

When you read this passage as it stands here, who is the subject?

Who does this passage speak about?

[197] They might also say that whilst Jesus reigns now, this is the beginning of his *bodily reign* on Earth.

In other words, who takes centre stage?

It's the followers of Jesus, right?

The ones who were killed for their faithfulness to Jesus are the subject of these verses. And if you're paying attention you'll see that Jesus is only mentioned incidentally.

And what does it say about them?

It says they came to life and reigned with Christ for a thousand years.

So who are the ones reigning for a thousand years?

It's those who follow Jesus.

The Christians.

So what point does this passage make?

It makes the point that faithful followers of Jesus will be raised to life and will reign with Christ for a thousand years.

And why is that interesting? Why is that a point worth making?

Because he was trying to say that those who were persecuted by Rome, who looked like the weak, defeated, pitiful ones in the eyes of the world who were cut down in the prime of their life because they wouldn't acknowledge Caesar is lord — now they come to life to reign with Christ (who has been shown to be the highest authority, moving all of history in accordance with his will) for a thousand years.

You see, if this is the message John was trying to convey then he did a great job doing it.

However, if John was trying to say that Jesus begins to reign for a thousand years, then I'm sure you'll admit he did a pretty poor job at communicating it.

My point is simply that we have made too much of 'the Millennium' and it's needs to be put into right proportion with the rest of the book of Revelation.

Personally, I don't believe this thousand years is literal. I believe it simply means a long time compared to the reign of the Caesars and even present day Presidents, Prime ministers, and despotic dictators. The point John makes is that the reward and benefit of following Jesus rather than capitulating to the worship and idolatry involved with following Caesar and the Empire (ancient, or present) is worth it.

Consequently, whenever the Millennium may be (past, present, or future), Jesus is presently reigning on Earth as in Heaven. Jesus is not Lord-elect, awaiting the day when he will be sworn in. All authority in Heaven and on Earth is already his. We are not waiting for a day in the future before we can expect the Lordship of Christ to be exercised and His Kingdom to be extended across our world.

We live within that reality right now.

I believe Jesus is Lord right now.

I believe all authority in Heaven and on Earth is His now.

I believe He is the King of all past, present, and future kings.

I believe this is God's world. This is not the devil's world. It used to be. But Jesus defeated, dethroned, and disarmed him.

I believe his Kingdom confronts the powers of our world whether they are political, economic, religious, or social and challenges their way of being and doing. What Jesus calls us to is not just a private spirituality.

I believe that this Kingdom is extending it's influence across our world and will continue to do so (albeit with opposition) until Jesus returns.

I believe all this because I believe Jesus is Lord.

What else could we possibly mean when we say that?

CHAPTER TWENTY-SIX

Great White Throne

Up until now we have covered a series of judgments:

- The 4 x 7 covenant judgment of the unfaithful house of Israel. This has already taken place.
- The beast (which is the Roman Empire) is judged. This has already taken place since the Roman Empire no longer exists.
- The whore of Babylon is judged. This is a judgment of the system of this world and it's final overthrow which I believe remains in the future.
- The red dragon is judged. This is Satan's judgment which has already taken place, but the carrying out of his sentence remains still future.
- These are the judgments of wicked oppressive systems and spiritual powers of evil.

But then John sees another final judgment. This is a personal judgment for each and every individual:

Then I saw a great white throne and him who was seated on it. From his presence earth and sky fled away, and no place was found for them. And I saw the dead, great and small, standing before the throne, and books were opened. Then another book was opened, which is the book of life. And the dead were judged by what was written in the books, according to what they had done. And the sea gave up the dead who were in it, Death and Hades gave up the dead who were in them, and they were judged, each one of them, according to what they had done. Then Death and Hades were thrown into the lake of fire. This is the second death, the lake of fire. And if anyone's name was not found written in the book of life, he was thrown into the lake of fire.[198]

I believe in a day of judgment.

I believe this world is a messed up place in so many deep ways, and I believe the God who created this world to be good will call each person to give an account for the way in which we have either partnered with him in redeeming this world or else contributed to it's brokenness. A good God will do no less.[199]

The Apostle Paul said,

[W]e will all stand before the judgment seat of God … each of us will give an account of himself to God.[200]

Elsewhere he says,

For we must all appear before the judgment seat of Christ, so that each one may receive what is due for what he has done in the body, whether good or evil.[201]

How do you feel when you read texts like these?

Afraid?

Hopeful?

---

[198] Revelation 20:11-15

[199] Remember that the emphasis of judgment is not first on retribution, but on restitution and redemption.

[200] Romans 14:10,12

[201] 2 Corinthians 5:10

Depending on how you feel you are doing will determine how you hear texts like these. However, if we are in Christ we should be able to face those texts with confidence:

So we have come to know and to believe the love that God has for us. God is love, and whoever abides in love abides in God, and God abides in him. By this is love perfected with us, so that we may have confidence for the day of judgment.[202]

If we abide in Christ, then we will have confidence as we look forward to the day of judgment. There shouldn't be a fear of hell or even of death because we know who we are, and we know who God is. In one sense our judgment has already taken place and we have been found to be in-the-right. That is what it means to be justified in Christ. It means our trial has already taken place and the verdict has been passed: not guilty.

However, the texts above speak about a judgment of rewards. They bring into the focus the fact that what we do with our lives matters to God. This should cause us to reflect soberly on what we are doing in our lives.

Listen to how the apostle Paul puts it:

According to the grace of God given to me, like a skilled master builder I laid a foundation, and someone else is building upon it. Let each one take care how he builds upon it. For no one can lay a foundation other than that which is laid, which is Jesus Christ. Now if anyone builds on the foundation with gold, silver, precious stones, wood, hay, straw — each one's work will become manifest, for the Day will disclose it, because it will be revealed by fire, and the fire will test what sort of work each one has done. If the work that anyone has built on the foundation survives, he will receive a reward. If anyone's work is burned up, he will suffer loss, though he himself will be saved, but only as through fire.[203]

---

[202] 1 John 4:16-17

[203] 1 Corinthians 3:10-15

The apostle Paul draws on the metaphor of a building when he writes to the church in the letter to the Corinthians and he speaks about two aspects of a building — the building and the foundation.

The foundation is Christ.

When we become followers of Jesus, he becomes our foundation. We may have built our lives on any number of different things which we once considered important or valuable. We may have built our lives on a dream we had or goals we wanted to achieve or a set of values. All of these things determine the shape the building takes.

But when we become followers of Jesus he becomes our foundation. He becomes the one who guides our life. He becomes the one who shapes the building and what it looks like. When the foundation of our life changes, parts of it may need some repair work, other parts may need to be completely vacated. This is the foundation which, if you are a follower of Jesus, is Christ Himself. And if this is the case we can have confidence on the Day of Judgment.

Then there is the building.

And those who build need to pay attention to how they build. Paul is making the point for those who work in building up God's people as overseers, but the point can be made for our own lives personally.

Each one of us has a responsibility to build on the foundation knowing that there will be a Day (capital "D" referring to Day of Judgment) when the quality of our work will be tested, and we will be rewarded or else suffer the loss of our reward. God will be like a divine building inspector and he will be looking for works done in faith and in love.

The Scriptures are clear in a number of places that there is reward for such works:

[W]hen you give to the needy, do not let your left hand know what your right hand is doing, so that your giving may be in secret. And your Father who sees in secret will reward you.[204]

Whatever you do, work heartily, as for the Lord and not for men, knowing that from the Lord you will receive the inheritance as your reward.[205]

If we live led by the Spirit of God, motivated by love and by faith, we are building with gold, silver and precious stones and there will be great reward. Dead works on the other hand are those which are done because we're trying to do good works so God will love us or accept us or will put God in our debt. They can be works that, if we are honest, are done to make us look good in the eyes of others. This is to build with wood, hay, and straw.

The fact that we will all stand before God and face judgment (not Heaven/Hell judgment, but reward/no reward judgment) should cause us to run our race with focus, determination, and perseverance, knowing that there is a reward waiting at the end of it all.

You've all been to the stadium and seen the athletes race. Everyone runs; one wins. Run to win. All good athletes train hard. They do it for a gold medal that tarnishes and fades. You're after one that's gold eternally.[206]

---

[204] Matthew 6:3-4

[205] Colossians 3:23-24

[206] 1 Corinthians 9:24-25 (MSG), emphasis added.

CHAPTER TWENTY-SEVEN

New Heavens and New Earth

We now turn our attention to the final vision given to us in Revelation:

Then I saw a new heaven and a new earth, for the first heaven and the first earth had passed away, and the sea was no more. And I saw the holy city, new Jerusalem, coming down out of heaven from God, prepared as a bride adorned for her husband. And I heard a loud voice from the throne saying, "Behold, the dwelling place of God is with man. He will dwell with them, and they will be his people, and God himself will be with them as their God. He will wipe away every tear from their eyes, and death shall be no more, neither shall there be mourning, nor crying, nor pain anymore, for the former things have passed away." And he who was seated on the throne said, "Behold, I am making all things new." Also he said, "Write this down, for these words are trustworthy and true."[207]

Here we see a number of startling things.

First, we do not see the destruction of Earth.

Earth is not destroyed, but made new: new Heavens and a new Earth.

But what about the Scripture where it says the world is going to be destroyed by fire?

[T]he heavens existed long ago, and the earth was formed out of water and through water by the word of God, and that by means of these the world that then existed

[207] Revelation 21:1-5

was deluged with water and perished. But by the same word the heavens and earth that now exist are stored up for fire, being kept until the day of judgment and destruction of the ungodly. … But the day of the Lord will come like a thief, and then the heavens will pass away with a roar, and the heavenly bodies will be burned up and dissolved, and the earth and the works that are done on it will be exposed. Since all these things are thus to be dissolved, what sort of people ought you to be in lives of holiness and godliness, waiting for and hastening the coming of the day of God, because of which the heavens will be set on fire and dissolved, and the heavenly bodies will melt as they burn! But according to his promise we are waiting for new heavens and a new earth in which righteousness dwells.[208]

This is the classic text which futurists claim teaches that the Earth is going to be annihilated.

But if you'll look closely, you'll see that it doesn't say that.

1. It doesn't say the Earth will be destroyed. It says the ungodly will be destroyed. It does say the heavenly bodies will be burned up and dissolved which could be a reference to the fact that in the new creation we will have no need for the Sun or the Moon because God himself will be the light.[209]

2. When Peter speaks about fire, as he does in his first letter, he speaks about it as a revealing and refining element rather than as a destructive one. So the point he makes here is not that Heaven and Earth will be consumed and annihilated, but rather nothing will remain hidden: "*the Earth and the works that are done on it will be exposed.*" Anything not of God will be burned up (like our dead works for example), and only that which is good and pure will make it through.

3. The word used here for "*new*" — as in "*new heavens and a new earth*" — is the Greek word *kainos*. In Greek, there are 2 words for new: *neos* and *kainos*. *Neos* is the idea of newness in bringing something to existence which hasn't

[208] 2 Peter 3:5-7, 10-13

[209] Revelation 21:23

existed before, whereas *kainos* is the idea of something which previously existed but has qualitatively been renewed.

4. If heaven and earth are to be destroyed rather than renewed, what sense would it make to encourage lives of holiness and godliness? Peter is using what he believes about the End Times as a means to encourage faithful living in this world rather than a detached form of escapism which leaves no impetus for godly living. If Peter believed the Earth would be destroyed together with all it's works, it was a terrible argument to use to make his point for Godly living.

5. The context is that the earth was once destroyed with water, in the future it will be destroyed with fire. I'm sure we're acquainted with the story of Noah's Ark and the flood. The flood didn't destroy the Earth, it purged it, cleansed it, and renewed it. It gave Noah and God a clean slate, a blank canvas from which to create a new world. This is precisely what Peter intends for us to understand when he talks about the End Times. He is speaking of renewing not annihilation.

Coming back to our text in Revelation:

Second, rather than the destruction of the Earth we see a renewal of both Heaven and Earth. The words from God's mouth are: "*I am making all things new.*" God is in the business of redeeming and renewing. He is not making all new things. He is making *all things new*. And that makes all the difference. Paul says of this present world:

For the creation waits with eager longing for the revealing of the sons of God. For the creation was subjected to futility, not willingly, but because of him who subjected it, in hope that the creation itself will be set free from its bondage to corruption and obtain the freedom of the glory of the children of God. For we know that the whole creation has been groaning together in the pains of childbirth until now.[210]

[210] Romans 8:19-22

One of the fundamental laws which governs our present reality is the law of entropy. The law of entropy essentially means that things always decay and lose energy. Just look around you and you'll see entropy at work — buildings slowly falling apart, cars rusting, our own bodies ageing — things by nature do not go from a state of disorder to order, but always in the opposite direction: from order to disorder.

But this is only true for our present age.

This will not be true in the age to come.

In this present age, Paul says that it is as though Creation itself is in bondage to corruption and decay. But one day it will be gloriously released from this bondage and will no longer be subject to the laws of entropy. Creation itself will receive the breath of immortality from the Lord of life himself, and will itself enter into the glory of the children of God. God will renew all of creation in an astounding way.

This hope of a renewed creation and resurrection bodies is true not only of the New Testament writings, but is in accord with the hopes of the ancient Jews as well:

[M]ainline Jews were not hoping to escape from the present universe into some Platonic realm of eternal bliss enjoyed by disembodied souls after the end of the space-time universe. If they died in the fight for the restoration of Israel, they hoped not to 'go to heaven', or at least not permanently, but to be raised to new bodies when the kingdom came, since they would of course need new bodies to enjoy the very much this-worldly shalom, peace and prosperity that was in store.[211]

Third, we see that rather than us going up into Heaven to dwell with God, God descends from Heaven to dwell with us. This means that while in the present

[211] N.T. Wright, *New Testament and the People of God*, pg. 286. If you want to read more on this subject of new Heaven and new Earth and the resurrection, you have to check out Tom Wright's book *Surprised by Hope*.

arrangement there seems to be some degree of separation between Heaven and Earth, in the new arrangement Heaven and Earth will be joined together.

What then did Jesus mean when he said to his disciples:

In my Father's house are many rooms. If it were not so, would I have told you that I go to prepare a place for you? And if I go and prepare a place for you, I will come again and will take you to myself, that where I am you may be also.[212]

How does the vision of Revelation make sense of the words of Jesus here?

Well, the fact is, we are already with Jesus. We are in Christ[213], Christ is in us[214], and we are seated with him in Heavenly places[215]. The Spirit of Christ lives in us[216], as does the Father[217]. Jesus therefore wasn't referring to a future existence in Heaven one day when we die, but to a present existence made possible here and now. When he said he would come again he was referring to the coming of the Holy Spirit who he said was just like himself.

Fourth, in this new arrangement of new Heavens and new Earth, John notes there is no more sea. This could mean the actual oceans of our planet, but I don't think so. I believe there is a better explanation offered by N.T. Wright. The Jews were not a sea faring nation by-and-large, and in their literature you can see how the sea often represents some form of mystery, danger, and even a source of evil (for example, Daniel saw a vision of beasts arising out of the sea). What John sees is the mysterious source of danger and evil no longer present in God's new world. This means we don't have to worry about evil and pain and

[212] John 14:2-3

[213] Philippians 1:1

[214] Colossians 1:27

[215] Ephesians 2:6

[216] 1 Corinthians 3:16

[217] John 14:23

death in the renewed world which God will make because it will no longer have any elements of evil which makes this present age so difficult and painful to us.

CHAPTER TWENTY-EIGHT

Selah

We've covered a lot of ground these last few chapters. Time for a brief recap:

- Revelation is written in a style called apocalyptic literature. It was not intended to be read literally.
- The book of Revelation is about Jesus.
- Large portions of Revelation give perspectives to the judgments of Jesus upon Israel and mirror what Jesus spoke about in Matthew 24.
- The beast is symbolic of the Roman Empire with it's current head being Caesar Nero.
- The antichrist is not a single world figure but a spirit/teaching (most likely Gnosticism) which plagued the early church.
- The Whore of Babylon represents the seductive power of empire which the people of God must resist.
- The Millennium is not necessarily a literal 1000 years, nor does that text make Jesus the focal point. Rather it is a text which encourages the saints of God to remain faithful even in the face of persecution.
- There will come a day when God will judge the world and everyone in it. Each person will receive their reward.
- At the consummation of the age, Heaven and Earth will be joined together as one. We are not anticipating Earth's final destruction, but rather it's renewal.

Here are some questions for you to consider:

How has your understanding of Revelation changed?

Is there less fear and anxiety?

Should you live in fear of God's coming judgment?

Is the seductive power of the empire expressed in Western culture something you are aware of?

How have you/will you seek to follow the Lamb rather than the way of the Whore of Babylon?

PART 4

So Now What?

CHAPTER TWENTY-NINE

Life After Death

My guess is if you've come this far you're probably wondering:

So the 'end times' are not what I've always thought them to be.

You might say to yourself:

If I think about it, we're living in a post-apocalyptic world.

That's a great thought there!

So what happens next? I mean, if all that is in the past, what lies in my future?

Great question.

Let's begin by talking about what happens after you die.

Paul the apostle said this:

"...it is my eager expectation and hope that I will not be at all ashamed, but that with full courage now as always Christ will be honored in my body, whether by life or by death. For to me to live is Christ, and to die is gain. If I am to live in the flesh, that means fruitful labor for me. Yet which I shall choose I cannot tell. I am hard pressed between the two. My desire is to depart and be with Christ, for that is far better. But to remain in the flesh is more necessary on your account. Convinced of this, I know

that I will remain and continue with you all, for your progress and joy in the faith..."[218]

For Paul he knew that to depart this life is to be with Christ. To remain in this life is to, "*remain in the flesh*" — in other words in his physical body. But to depart is to leave his physical body behind and enter a different kind of existence. An existence in which we remain conscious and in the presence of the Lord.

Right now we enjoy a measure of connection with God, but after we die we will enjoy unbroken, unhindered connection with Him. While you are alive now, you might really love the way things are, but if Paul was asked to make a choice between staying in this present existence or departing and going to be with Jesus, he said it would be tough to choose. On the one hand, to be with Jesus is amazing, but to remain here is to enjoy fruitful labour, serving and loving God by serving and loving his people.

I believe Paul's tension is a healthy one.

Would you feel the same way? Do you live with this tension?

On the one hand do you know there is meaning and purpose to your life here and now?

Can you connect what you do here and now as you serve and love people with actually loving and serving God?[219]

Is there fruitfulness to your present existence?

Are you engaging in the good works which God has prepared for you to do?

On the other hand, do you long for the day when you will be united with Christ?

---

[218] Philippians 1:20-25

[219] For a great book on this subject check out *Garden City* by John Mark Comer.

Do you hold the things of this world lightly knowing there will be a day when you will leave them behind — even your body behind — and go to be with Jesus?

Paul felt this tension and it is a healthy one for us to cultivate.

All those who die in Christ will leave this present existence to be with Jesus in a Heavenly existence. Many believe this is where the story of eternity ends. But this is not where the Bible says it ends.

For many, they believe when Jesus returns He does so with a view to rapture all believers off the planet, take them off to Heaven, and pour his wrath out on the planet Earth until it's final destruction. We will then go on to live a disembodied spiritual existence in Heaven for all eternity.

Playing harps.

Or singing.

Or something boring like that.

But I have a couple of problems with this (you probably figured this out already).

If that *is* what you believe, what point is there in making any difference in this world here and now?

Who cares about global warming?

Who cares about saving the Rhinos?

Who cares about better education?

Who cares about feeding the poor?

Who cares about addressing systemic injustice and oppression?

Let's just get people saved!

Let's get them ready for Heaven!

After all, this is all going to burn anyway.

It's souls that matter.

The trouble is, for Jesus, it wasn't just souls that mattered. Furthermore, it wasn't just the individual person he came to fix. He confronted evil in all it's forms, including the dark force of evil itself — the satan. It was the devil who had enslaved people who together had ruined God's good world. The whole cosmos mattered to Jesus which is why he addressed evil head on and defeated it at the Cross.[220] His purpose was the redemption of *all things* and the summing up of *all things* in Christ.[221]

Why then would God just surrender this good world which he made into the hands of the devil in the end?

Jesus wasn't as interested about getting people into Heaven as he was about getting Heaven into us.

And then from us into this world.

His divine intent is for Earth to be flooded with Heaven.

---

220 Colossians 2:15

221 Ephesians 1:10

This is the vision of the Old Testament prophets: that the Earth would be filled with the glory of the Lord.[222]

That reality is already present in Christ and his Church, and it will be finally present when Earth and Heaven are finally brought together.

So what does this all mean for me? 2 texts will help us, one from Paul's letter to the Thessalonians and the other from Corinthians:

But we do not want you to be uninformed, brothers, about those who are asleep, that you may not grieve as others do who have no hope. For since we believe that Jesus died and rose again, even so, through Jesus, God will bring with him those who have fallen asleep. For this we declare to you by a word from the Lord, that we who are alive, who are left until the coming of the Lord, will not precede those who have fallen asleep. For the Lord himself will descend from heaven with a cry of command, with the voice of an archangel, and with the sound of the trumpet of God. And the dead in Christ will rise first. Then we who are alive, who are left, will be caught up together with them in the clouds to meet the Lord in the air, and so we will always be with the Lord. Therefore encourage one another with these words.[223]

Behold! I tell you a mystery. We shall not all sleep, but we shall all be changed, in a moment, in the twinkling of an eye, at the last trumpet. For the trumpet will sound, and the dead will be raised imperishable, and we shall be changed. For this perishable body must put on the imperishable, and this mortal body must put on immortality.[224]

Paul says the trumpet will sound and Jesus will return. When Jesus returns he will bring with him those who have already died. In other words, those who are currently with Jesus will appear with him at the end, and their bodies will rise

[222] See Numbers 14:21, Psalm 72:19, Habakkuk 2:14

[223] 1 Thessalonians 4:13-18

[224] 1 Corinthians 15:51-53

from the Earth as renewed resurrection bodies — like that of Jesus'. Up until this point they have been in Heaven in a purely 'spiritual' existence, but when Jesus returns they will receive their resurrection bodies — a physical body like the body which Jesus Himself received upon his resurrection. In some way it resembles the old one but is made gloriously new. It will be a physical body but without the effects of ageing or decay. As strange as it sounds and as difficult as it may be to comprehend, it will be an *eternal physicality*.

We who are alive, who remain until the Lord returns, will be changed. In that moment our present bodies will be transformed to be like his glorious body and we too will possess the fullness of resurrection life as Jesus does. The perishable will have been put off and we would have been clothed with the imperishable.

This will be the final state of the believer. We will not exist in a purely 'spiritual' form for all eternity. Rather, we will possess a body of eternal physicality that will not grow old.

Why is this important?

Because we will need a resurrected, renewed physical body so we may inhabit God's new world which he will make as he brings together not just the spiritual nature of Heaven but also the physical nature of Earth. Heaven and Earth itself will be joined together. New Heavens and new Earth, something neither has yet fully experienced except in Jesus himself as the foretaste of what is to come.

Because we'll have resurrected bodies to inhabit the new Heaven and new Earth, all kinds of things become possible. We will still find meaningful work to do. Many of the things we do in this life we may still do in the next — only with greater joy and purpose. We don't know what it will be like, we just know it will be wonderful. It will be life and life abundant.

Life after life after death.[225]

---

[225] Tom Wright, *Surprised by Hope*, location 2544 (Kindle edition)

To summarise: if you are in Christ, upon death you enter into a new kind of existence: life after death. But when Jesus brings about the consummation of the ages and returns, there will be a new kind of existence, the renewal of Heaven and Earth and the joining together of the two where we will receive resurrection bodies: it will be life after life after death. The Earth will not be destroyed or discarded, it will be renewed. God will ultimately redeem all things.[226] This is thoroughly Biblical and faithful to both Old and New Testaments.

---

[226] There does of course remain the question of Hell and Purgatory which I will not tackle here.

CHAPTER THIRTY

Life Before Death

So you've got to the end of my book.

Congratulations.

Now what?

What do we do with all this information?

How does it change the way I live here and now?

Great questions.

What we believe about the end times definitely shapes the way we live here, now, today. If you don't believe me, just flip over to the National Geographic Channel and watch *Doomsday Preppers.* Here you will find people who believe there will come, within their lifetime, some biological war, or nuclear holocaust, or zombie apocalypse, and when it comes they will be ready with their underground bunkers, food stashes, guns and ammunition. Of course most of us believe that these people are more than a little paranoid, but the truth is we all live and make decisions today based on what we believe the future will look like — whether we realise it or not.

So you may disagree with everything in this book.

I guess I'm ok with that. We probably shouldn't be too dogmatic on these matters.

However.

How do your beliefs affect the way you live here and now? Because what I find is that bad beliefs on the End Times lead to bad behaviour. And if there are behavioural patterns that are somehow supported by a bad belief system, then you've taken a wrong turn somewhere and you need to head back and ask for direction.

So if your theory on the End Times leads you to demonise people (frequently labelling this president, or that business leader, as the antichrist for example) then perhaps you've taken a wrong turn somewhere.

If your theory of the End Times leads you to believe that God favours war in the Middle East over peace, and that in fact peace in the Middle East is a sign of the devil at work, you've taken a wrong turn somewhere.

If your theory of the End Times leads you toward an escapist posture where you are just looking forward to the rapture when you will get to leave all this mess behind, you've taken a wrong turn somewhere.

If your theory of the End Times causes you to live in fear, you've taken a wrong turn somewhere.

In the previous chapter we dealt with life after death. This one will be focused on life *before* death. We'll deal with the question of what we are to do here and now because of what we believe about the End Times and the future of all things.

Let's talk about the Pope.[227] Pope John Paul II was asked by a journalist once, *"what would you say if you knew Jesus was coming back tomorrow?" "Look busy,"* he replied with a grin.

[227] Yup, we're talking about the Pope again.

I believe Jesus is coming back. There is a lot which has already happened (as I have laboured to point out) but that doesn't mean Jesus isn't coming back. He is.

Right now, in the present arrangement, we experience pain and loss and grief, but one day these will all come to an end. They won't come to an end because Jesus will whisk us off into Heaven. It'll come to an end because Jesus will consummate his Kingdom on Earth as it is in Heaven. Death will be swallowed up by life. That is the Christian hope. But it isn't a passive hope. We don't sit on our hands waiting for that day. We have a task given to us by the Master.

First, we have been given the task to be witnesses.

A major theme throughout Revelation is Jesus is Lord (and Caesar is not). Jesus reigns (and the satan does not). This means the world is different because of what he did almost 2000 years ago on that Cross.

We are called to bear witness to that change in word and in deed.

As we live led and empowered by his Spirit, as we worship our Father, and as we follow Jesus, we bear witness to the fact that Jesus is Lord and the world is under new management.[228] We bear witness in our families and communities and workplaces and schools and universities.

We bear witness when we live as though God's reality is the ultimate reality. That taking second place (or last place) is actually taking first place in God's economy of things. This is what Jesus meant when he said if we wanted to be the greatest we must become the servant. What if he was right? I mean, what if everyone has been chasing greatness, but they've been going in the opposite direction? Can you even begin to imagine this possibility? Because if you can, then you have a glimpse of the Kingdom reality Jesus calls us to bear faithful witness to.

---

[228] If you want to read an excellent book on this check out *Simply Good News* by Tom Wright.

We live as though giving is better than getting. Because it is. Even if the world thinks it isn't. This is how we bear witness to the upside-down-ness of God's new arrangement of the world (which Jesus called the Kingdom).

We bear witness to this Kingdom by believing and acting as though loving our enemies is better than hating them, cursing them, and bombing them. When the world plays it's familiar marching beat of exclusion and fear, we bear witness to this Kingdom by sitting around a table with the "other" and sharing a meal and a story.

We bear witness by believing and acting as though turning the other cheek is better than retaliating. "*I don't want a battle from beginning to end, I don't want a cycle of recycled revenge, I don't want to follow death and all of his friends.*"[229] Instead, we put an end to recycled revenge by forgiving and pronouncing peace.[230] We bear witness when we believe and act as though forgiving is better than revenge.

We bear witness when we value people more than things. In a world which will spend money on their pet's health insurance before it will do it for their domestic worker, we have an opportunity to adjust the terms and conditions of the status quo.

Jesus changed the world, and we are called to bear witness to that change with our lives.

Second, we have been called to fruitful labour.

In 1 Corinthians 15 Paul lays out his belief around death, and what lies beyond the grave. It is his most systematic and comprehensive thinking on the subject which we have in the Bible. After a lengthy chapter writing about it he ends off by saying:

---

[229] A great line from a great band. Coldplay, *Death and All His Friends*.

[230] John 20:19

Therefore, my beloved brothers, be steadfast, immovable, always abounding in the work of the Lord, knowing that in the Lord your labor is not in vain.[231]

Your labour is not in vain.

Is that the way you would end a chapter on life after death and the resurrection hope? If it had been me, I might have said something like:

"Don't worry about how difficult things get down here because it'll all come to an end someday and then you'll go to Heaven."

Or,

"Hey, don't put too much effort into Earthly work, after all it's all going to burn."

But Paul sees it fundamentally differently. Rather than seeing a disconnection between what happens here and now and what happens there and then, he sees connection. He sees that somehow our work here and now has value into eternity. He sees the work we do here and now motivated by love for God and for people, will somehow mysteriously make its way into the new world which God will make.

Your labour in the Lord is not in vain.

Therefore we can't be people who just 'let things be'.

Jesus won't let us be those kind of people.

Christians are not people who look at the way the world is and say, '*meh*'. We have a purpose here and now which involves bringing about the same kind of change as that which Jesus brought. He didn't look at sickness and say, "*Don't*

---

[231] 1 Corinthians 15:58

worry, if you die from this at least you'll go to Heaven." He didn't look at injustice and oppression and say, "*Hey I know things are hard now, but one day when you die it will be better.*"

Jesus ultimately gave his life to put an end to death and all his friends:[232] injustice, oppression, sickness, violence, racism, revenge, and greed, amongst others. He gave his life as a ransom for many, so that every one of us might be set free from the enslaving power of sin, set free from unquestioned allegiance to the Empire (whatever shape it may take). He did it so we could step into the purpose which God had marked out for us from the beginning: to be those who bear his image in the world — ruling and reigning and extending his order and shalom across the world in a truly human way.

The Gospel knows nothing of the attitude which sits back waiting for the mothership to arrive and beam us up out of here. We, who are called 'new creations', are called to bring about signs and foretastes of God's new creation wherever we might find ourselves, whether it be behind an office desk, espresso machine, hospital nursing station, taxi steering wheel, or serving apron.

Tom Wright puts it so well:

[W]hat you do in the Lord is not in vain. You are not oiling the wheels of a machine that's about to fall over a cliff. You are not restoring a great painting that's shortly going to be thrown on the fire. You are not planting roses in a garden that's about to be dug up for a building site. You are – strange though it may seem, almost as hard to believe as the resurrection itself – accomplishing something which will become, in due course, part of God's new world. Every act of love, gratitude and kindness; every work of art or music inspired by the love of God and delight in the beauty of his creation; every minute spent teaching a severely handicapped child to read or to walk; every act of care and nurture, of comfort and support, for one's fellow human beings, and for that matter one's fellow non-human creatures; and of course every prayer, all Spirit-led teaching, every deed which spreads the gospel, builds up the

[232] A nod to Coldplay again.

church, embraces and embodies holiness rather than corruption, and makes the name of Jesus honoured in the world – all of this will find its way, through the resurrecting power of God, into the new creation which God will one day make. That is the logic of the mission of God.[233]

So. Good.

Third, we are salt and light *in* the world — but not *of* the world.

When Jesus was questioned by Pilate he said, "*My kingdom is not of this world.*"[234] What he *wasn't* saying is that his Kingdom has nothing to do with this world. What he *was* saying is that his Kingdom didn't originate in this world, but it is certainly *for* this world.

Jesus said his disciples were salt and light. However we may interpret these metaphors, one thing is clear: proximity and visibility. We are to be in the world for the sake of influencing it.

In my country of South Africa, however, we have too many theological frameworks which enable us to get out of this world, or at least keep it at arms length.[235] For example:

We get promised a ticket to Heaven when we die with little concern with how we live here and now.

The Gospel is spiritualised so it has almost nothing to say about much of the 'stuff' of everyday life — whether politics, economics, racism, and the education crisis amongst others.

---

[233] Tom Wright, *Surprised by Hope*, location 3413 (Kindle edition)

[234] John 18:36

[235] Thanks to Jana Niehaus for her insight here.

We are taught about a coming rapture which means we'll get out of here in the nick of time just before the Earth is completely destroyed. "Just live a holy life so you won't be Left Behind."

We are taught that we will never have to suffer hardship and if we have enough faith we can live healthy and wealthy.

These are just a few examples which I'm sure are not unique to us in South Africa. Too often we have been peddled a thin, watered down Gospel that is so paltry and emaciated it is hardly recognisable alongside the glorious, just, big, shalom-bringing, all-of-creation-redeeming story that is the Good News of the Kingdom of God.

This has been my point all along. Our belief on the End Times need to reflect this bigness. It needs to be more buoyant and hopeful *because our Gospel is*. And so maybe for you nothing really changes. Perhaps all that's changed is that you've actually resolved some of your misalignment, and your beliefs on the End Times have now finally aligned with something you are already living and believing. Maybe all I've given you is vocabulary for something you've felt and thought for a long time. If that's the case: awesome.

But hopefully for others, this changes everything.

Maybe you can finally start imagining what it would look like to engage in this world beyond the saving-souls-for-heaven level.

Maybe your eyes are beginning to be opened to a Gospel which is Good News of great joy *for all people*. A Gospel which is politically subversive, economically revolutionary, and socially transformative. A Gospel which is conversant with the world out there as it is in it's difficulties, challenges, and mess. And a Jesus who is up to the task.

Maybe you're an engineer, or gym instructor, or teacher, or domestic worker, or accountant, or mechanic, or cook, or businessperson, or stay at home mom. *How does this kind of Gospel enable you to take what you do and truly engage in the world as it is in all it's mess and confusion?*

How can you be part of the solution rather than part of the ongoing problem?

How can you begin to free yourself from captivity to the Empire of individuality, capitalism, and consumerism and instead live into a different Story? One which is more God honouring?

How can you do what you do every day in such a way that it adds value to the world and those around you?

How can you do it with integrity and a clear conscience?

How can you live God's future here and now?

How can you do it with a creative imagination which is open to the kaleidoscopic brilliance and Genius of Life that is God's Spirit?

How can you do it in a way that increases the shalom of our world — whether it be for people or for the environment?

Maybe you should get together with a few friends and start asking some of these questions and see where it takes you?

There is much work to be done. For too long too many have embraced sub-Gospel teachings which have crippled the Body of Christ in a paralysis of inaction while we wait for the rapture. We need healthy beliefs because beliefs always determine behaviours.

My hope is that this book has been able to offer you some better beliefs on the End Times so that we can become the kind of Church Jesus dreams of.

CHAPTER THIRTY-ONE

APPENDIX: Extra Credit

There are some things which I just know many people are not that interested in.

Then there is you.

You're here because you're looking for extra credit. Well done! Here you will find my nerdy details about timelines and prophetic details that most find tedious. Enjoy!

GOD'S FUTURE PLANS FOR THE JEWS

Whenever one's beliefs on the End Times are challenged, the thing people are often most concerned about is the place of Israel. If the End Times are not what we thought they were, then what does this mean for Israel?

Has God abandoned his people?

Is there any benefit in being a Jew?

To get fuller answers to these questions I direct you to Paul's letter to the Romans and find that these are all answered by him in turn.[236] I'm not going to repeat his arguments here, but let me say a few things.

[236] See Romans 3:1 and chapters 9-11 (esp. 11:1)

First, God has one plan for all people (for both Jews and Gentiles) which has been unveiled in Christ. There is not one way of salvation for Gentiles and a different way for Jews. Both must find redemption in Christ. This means God's plan cannot be to reconstruct a physical temple in Jerusalem as a way to bring the Jewish story to a conclusion. Jesus is the new Temple and his body — those who trust and follow him — are the living stones being built together into a dwelling of God by his Spirit.[237] All the promises of God find their yes and amen in Christ.[238] This means the promises to the Jews are not awaiting their fulfilment — they have already been fulfilled in Christ.

Some have labelled this particular perspective '*replacement theology*'. For anyone who has been paying attention to everything I have said in this book I offer a better term: '*fulfilment theology*'. Israel hasn't been sidelined, rather, Jesus has brought their Law and Prophets to fulfilment and carried them forward in his person. The people of God (which now include all nations) are constituted around his person rather than around a national identity.

Secondly, God's plan is to reconcile the Jews to himself in Christ. He has not forgotten about them, discarded them, or replaced them. Jews are not second rate citizens in the Kingdom and in God's plan of redemption. True Jews[239] will find their place again in God's family, only this time no longer oriented around a national identity, circumcision, Temple, geography, or the Law, but around Jesus.

Thirdly, regarding timelines, it seems to me this process of reconciliation is not reserved for some day in the future. To phrase it as a question: will the Jews only be converted in the End Times, perhaps when the Christians have been 'Raptured' to heaven? All we have is one scripture to go by where Paul says that there will indeed be a future element to their reintegration into the people of

---

[237] 1 Peter 2:5

[238] 2 Corinthians 1:20

[239] Romans 9:6

God,[240] but this mercy is available for them to receive even now.[241] A partial hardening has taken place yet even now many Jews have come to faith in Jesus here and now. We as Christians would do well to learn from them and allow them to deepen and enrich our faith.

All things considered I think it is a mistake to centre one's reading of the End Times around Israel. Israel is not 'God's clock' (as Irvin Baxter,[242] amongst others, has put it), as though we can get an idea of the 'time' based on what is taking place in Israel and Jerusalem. God has centred all things on Jesus. He is the one around whom all of history is turning and Israel must find their proper place around him.

DANIEL'S 70 WEEKS

According to the prophetic writings of Daniel, there was to be a prince, the anointed one, or in Hebrew, the Messiah, who was expected to appear within a particular timeframe. It reads:

"Seventy weeks have been decreed for your people and your holy city, to finish the transgression, to make an end of sin, to make atonement for iniquity, to bring in everlasting righteousness, to seal up vision and prophecy and to anoint the most holy place. So you are to know and discern that from the issuing of a decree to restore and rebuild Jerusalem until Messiah the Prince there will be seven weeks and sixty-two weeks; it will be built again, with plaza and moat, even in times of distress. Then after the sixty-two weeks the Messiah will be cut off and have nothing, and the people of the prince who is to come will destroy the city and the sanctuary. And its end will come with a flood; even to the end there will be war; desolations are determined. And he will make a firm covenant with the many for one week, but in the middle of the week he will put a stop to sacrifice and grain offering;

240 Romans 11:25

241 Romans 11:31

242 See www.endtime.com

and on the wing of abominations will come one who makes desolate, even until a complete destruction, one that is decreed, is poured out on the one who makes desolate."[243]

Each "week" in this text represents seven years (most commentators agree on this), which makes seventy "weeks" equal to four hundred and ninety years. There is much in this text which requires explanation but let us keep to that which is pertinent for the topic at hand.

What Daniel sees is the coming of an anointed one — a prince — but he sees a period of time before his appearing. The period given is 49 years plus 434 years which totals 483 years. But there is a catch. This clock doesn't start until the time a decree is issued to rebuild Jerusalem. So in short, the anointed one (the Messiah) will appear 483 years after a decree is issued to rebuild Jerusalem.

When was such a decree issued? It was issued by Artaxerxes the king of Persia to Ezra the priest[244] in the seventh year of his rule. According to historical records,[245] Artaxerxes began his reign in either 465 or 464 B.C.E (depending on which counting method was used). Adding seven to this gives us 458 or 457 B.C.E. This is the date when the decree was issued. Adding on Daniel's sixty nine weeks (483 years) gives us 26 or 27 A.D. (keeping in mind there is no year '0').

27 A.D. is within the timeframe within which Jesus is supposed to have started his ministry, three years later he was crucified (30 A.D.) and within a generation (40 years) Jerusalem was destroyed (70 A.D.) The timeline fits.

The reason this is so important is because there were many others doing the maths too. Probably more than any other point in history, the Jews anticipated the arrival of Messiah any moment because that is where Daniel's seventy weeks

243 Daniel 9:24-27 (NASB)

244 See Ezra 7:11-20

245 For example, the Greek historian Ptolemy's Canon

had led them. It should come as no surprise then that anyone with a little bit of ambition would take that time as the opportunity to make a name for themselves to claim the title of 'Messiah' and lead a rebellion against the Romans. This is what some did indeed do.

What about Daniel's final 'week'? Many futurist teachers say there is a massive gap between week 69 and week 70. They teach that the final 7 years are still to come, during which time the great tribulation will occur. There is no reason to interpret this text in that way. There is no logical reason to insert a massive gap (2000 years and growing) between Daniel's 69th and 70th week. Rather; there is more support to say that the desolations and the end of sacrifice decreed in the 70th week, happened shortly after the coming of the anointed one (Jesus) in 70 A.D.

WHAT ABOUT DOUBLE FULFILMENT?

When Jerusalem was destroyed in 70 A.D. all that Jesus had spoken prophetically about Jerusalem and the Temple was fulfilled. One might ask at this point whether a double fulfilment is possible. For those unfamiliar with this term, in Scripture we sometimes see a prophetic message being filled (occurring at one time in history), and then filled again (occurring at another time in history), until finally it is filled to the full — i.e. fulfilled (perhaps in the person of Jesus, or in the New Testament Church).

So one may be willing to concede that these signs may have already been fulfilled, but who is to say this isn't just *one instance* of them being filled? How can we say for sure that they will not be fully filled again at some future point? Could we then expect a cosmic apocalypse sometime in our future, characterised by the things Jesus spoke of in Matthew 24 and in Revelation?

I don't believe this is possible for one major reason from Matthew 23:

"You serpents, you brood of vipers, how are you to escape being sentenced to hell? Therefore I send you prophets and wise men and scribes, some of whom you will kill and crucify, and some you will flog in your synagogues and persecute from town to town, so that on you may come all the righteous blood shed on earth, from the blood of righteous Abel to the blood of Zechariah the son of Barachiah, whom you murdered between the sanctuary and the altar. Truly, I say to you, all these things will come upon this generation.

O Jerusalem, Jerusalem, the city that kills the prophets and stones those who are sent to it! How often would I have gathered your children together as a hen gathers her brood under her wings, and you were not willing! See, your house is left to you desolate."[246]

Jesus spoke here of a judgment coming upon the generation of Jews to whom he was speaking, but it was no ordinary judgment. An ordinary judgment would have been a judgment on the basis of sin they were personally culpable for. But Jesus pronounces an extraordinary judgment in that all the innocent blood from Abel (these individuals could not have murdered Abel since they wouldn't have been born) to Zechariah (which they might have been involved in) would come upon them. It was a covenantal judgment upon a unfaithful nation.

All that follows in Matthew 24 as well as large portions of Revelation are based on this extraordinary covenantal judgment (the judgment of Leviticus 26) which would be unjust for God to repeat again at some point in the future. Thus I don't believe a double fulfilment of these signs is possible since they are based on an extraordinary judgment and signal a closing of the book (so to speak) on the Old Covenant. Simply put, these are non-repeatable events.

However, this doesn't mean that these texts have nothing to say to us. I believe they offer us a window into the events and the people who endured them. They warn us of the dangers of capitulating to an empire which wants to draw us away from devotion to the Lamb and into it's own dominating, selfish, and

[246] Matthew 23:33-38

oppressive narrative. We learn courage and patience from the examples of those who faced violent persecution and remained faithful to Jesus through it all. We learn that empires come and go, but the Kingdom of God is never shaken, it always endures, and it will one day be a mountain which fills the whole Earth.

WHEN WAS THE BOOK OF REVELATION WRITTEN?

It is important to know when the book of Revelation was written because if it was written after the fall of Jerusalem (70-73 A.D.) then it must refer to events beyond that. If however it was written before then, it could very well be writing about what was soon to take place during those terribly dark days.

It is my belief that John wrote this book sometime between 65 and 70A.D. There is some disagreement amongst scholars[247] on this but it seems to me there is enough evidence to support the dating of this book in that period.

Perhaps the first place to start is with the opening words of the book itself:

The revelation of Jesus Christ, which God gave him to show to his servants the things that must soon take place. … Blessed is the one who reads aloud the words of this prophecy, and blessed are those who hear, and who keep what is written in it, for the time is near.[248]

John is told that these things are "*soon*" to take place and that the time for the fulfilment of what is written in it is "*near*". On a plain reading of these words it would seem that John is not recording things which would take place in a long time (in 2000 years and counting), but will take place soon.

---

[247] For example, the introduction to the book of Revelation in the ESV version notes that Revelation was written between 95-96 A.D. The Expositors Bible Commentary notes that Irenaeus held to a late authorship (same as the ESV), whilst scholars such as Westcott, Hort, and Lightfoot held to an earlier dating.

[248] Revelation 1:1a, 3

In Revelation 11 John is told to measure the Temple:

Rise and measure the temple of God and the altar and those who worship there, but do not measure the court outside the temple; leave that out, for it is given over to the nations, and they will trample the holy city for forty-two months.[249]

For John to measure the Temple of God and those who worship there must mean that Temple is still standing and there are still people worshipping there. If this was written after 70 A.D. (i.e. Before the fall of Jerusalem) there would be no temple to measure, and no worshippers present. Furthermore, in this text, the "holy city" is still standing which means this must be before it's destruction.

One may argue that this is referring to a rebuilt Temple which still remains in the future, but then we must come back again to the opening words of the letter: "*soon*" and "*near*" not "*much later*" and "*far away*".

Furthermore, the 42 months during which time the Gentiles would trample the holy city was the same duration of the war against the Jews by the Romans. Vespasian was commissioned by Nero in February of A.D. 67, and the city fell in August under the command of Titus (Vespasian's son) in August of A.D. 70. This supports an earlier authorship of Revelation.

Then there is a vision in Revelation which overlaps very well with the history of the day:

And I saw a beast rising out of the sea, with ten horns and seven heads, with ten diadems on its horns and blasphemous names on its heads. And the beast that I saw was like a leopard; its feet were like a bear's, and its mouth was like a lion's mouth. And to it the dragon gave his power and his throne and great authority. One of its heads seemed to have a mortal wound, but its mortal wound was healed, and the whole earth marvelled as they followed the beast. And they worshiped the

---

[249] Revelation 11:1-2

dragon, for he had given his authority to the beast, and they worshiped the beast, saying, "Who is like the beast, and who can fight against it?"[250]

The interpretation of this vision comes 4 chapters later:

But the angel said to me … "I will tell you the mystery … of the beast with seven heads and ten horns … the seven heads are seven mountains on which the woman is seated; they are also seven kings, five of whom have fallen, one is, the other has not yet come, and when he does come he must remain only a little while. … And the ten horns that you saw are ten kings who have not yet received royal power, but they are to receive authority as kings for one hour, together with the beast."[251]

The information we have is this: the beast represents seven mountains and it represents seven kings. What could that mean? One possible interpretation is that this represents Rome since it is a city with it's famed seven mountains.[252] It wouldn't be going too far to say that the beast on one hand represents Rome and the Roman Empire.

Second, we are told the seven heads also represent seven kings, five have fallen, one is, and one is still to come but only for a short while. If we assume an earlier dating of the book of Revelation (sometime around the early to mid 60's), Caesar Nero would have been in power. Which means from the beginning of the Julio-Claudian line of emperors, 5 Caesars had fallen, one was (Nero), and one was still to come but for a short while. History will show that Caesar Galba who followed Nero reigned for only 7 months in what came to be known in history as the year of 4 emperors.[253]

---

[250] Revelation 13:1-4

[251] Revelation 17:7-12

[252] There was even a movie in the 1950's by the name Seven Hills of Rome.

[253] The information in the table below is readily available online.

CAESAR	
Julius	49 BC – 44 BC
Augustus	27 BC – 14 AD
Tiberius	14–37 AD
Caligula	37–41 AD
Claudius	41–54 AD
Nero	54–68 AD
Galba	68–69 AD (7 months)

John goes on to say:

And the beast was given a mouth uttering haughty and blasphemous words, and it was allowed to exercise authority for forty-two months. … Also it was allowed to make war on the saints and to conquer them. … Here is a call for the endurance and faith of the saints.[254]

In A.D. 64, a fire broke out in Rome destroying a third of the city. Some believed Nero himself had set the fire, but Nero blamed the Christians. This began a period of intense persecution which continued under Nero until his death 3 and a half years later, which is 42 months.

From this I conclude that the beast in Revelation was the Roman Empire ruled at that time by Caesar Nero. Overlaying these visions with history reveals a neat alignment, and supports an earlier authorship.

I believe the mortal head wound which had been healed referred to the upheaval which followed Nero's sudden suicide. His death marked the end of the Julio-Claudian line of emperors which had begun with Julius Caesar. Following Nero's death, the Roman Empire had 4 emperors in a single year. It was a time when it looked as though Rome would crumble under the weight of infighting and civil

[254] Revelation 13:5-10

war — that Rome itself might fall. Vespasian however, managed to bring things under control and restored peace, establishing a new line of the Flavian dynasty, reviving the Empire.

As a final point, the Classical Syriac version of the New Testament (sometimes called the Syriac Vulgate or the Peshitta) states on the opening page of the book of Revelation: "*The Revelation, which was made by God to John the Evangelist, in the Island of Patmos, To which he was banished by Nero the Emperor.*"[255] This could only have taken place before Nero's death which was pre-70 A.D.

In light of all this it seems to me that an earlier dating of the book of Revelation (somewhere in the early to mid 60's) is preferable. This therefore opens up the possibility that part of the unfolding of Revelation refers to the fall of Jerusalem.

Here are some words which are associated with the End Times. The only theory I am in agreement with is Partial Preterism.

DISPENSATIONALISM

Dispensationalism is a particular way of understanding the Scriptures and God's plan for his world. Simply put, those who are Dispensationalists believe that God has dealt with different groups of people in clearly defined 'dispensations'. In the first dispensation he has dealt with Israel. The first coming of Jesus signalled the end of this first dispensation and marked the beginning of the second dispensation, which is God's current dealings with the church. The final dispensation will be when God finally returns to conclude his work with Israel before the end of the world.

---

[255] https://www.originalbibles.com/peshitta-syriac-middle-aramaic-new-testament-1915-pdf/ (see page 491)

MILLENNIALISM

In Revelation 20, John has a vision of the reign of Christ which would last a thousand years. This has come to be known as the 'Millennium'. What one believes about the Millennium (When does it start? How long is it exactly? Are we to take it literally?) divides the main theories on the 'End Times'. If one holds to 'premillennialism', for example, they hold to the belief Christ will return before the start of the thousand years.

RAPTURE

'Rapture' theory exists exclusively among premillennials (those who believe Christ will return before the thousand year reign of Revelation 20), and is the belief that believers will be secretly caught up into Heaven by God before the final judgment. This will leave the remaining wicked on Earth which will then be ripe for God's punishment and wrath.

TRIBULATION

In Matthew and Revelation, we encounter the concept of 'Tribulation' which, according to adherents, will be a time of great suffering for many on the earth for a period of seven years. This word functions alongside 'Rapture' to designate when believers will be raptured—before the Tribulation begins (pre-tribulation Rapture), in the middle of the Tribulation (mid-tribulation Rapture), or (God help us) we stick around for the whole thing (post-tribulation Rapture).

DISPENSATIONAL PREMILLENNIALISM

Currently, this is the most popular of the End Times theories. The origins of Dispensationalism, Rapture theory, and the Tribulation in particular can be traced back to the teachings of the Englishman J.N. Darby (1800-1882), who was one of the founding fathers of the Plymouth Brethren movement. He had been influenced by a revelation from a lady named Margaret MacDonald in which she claimed to have seen Christ coming secretly before his second coming in order to rapture a special group of believers to Heaven.[256] Darby is purported to have borrowed from her, modifying her views, and then taught them as his own. This idea, combined with the seventy weeks of Daniel (Daniel 9:24-27) formed what came to be known as Dispensationalism. He brought his views across to America around 1864 where it grew in popularity, until Darby's ideas were included in the footnotes of the Scofield Reference Bible published first in 1909. This Bible was unique in it's time as it included the Biblical text alongside a scholarly commentary (the first to do so since the Geneva Bible published in 1560). This made it a very popular choice amongst pastors and people alike, and thus the ideas of Dispensationalism and Rapture theory were disseminated to the masses. Stan Newton writes, "*The Scofield Bible has probably done more to spread the cause of dispensationalism than any other entity.*"[257] Later, Finis Dake followed in the tradition of Darby's Dispensationalism and published Dake's Annotated Reference Bible which included his personal notes alongside the Biblical text.

Since that time Darby's Dispensational teaching has found numerous expressions in Christian culture. Edgar Whisenant sold 4.5 million copies of his book *88 Reasons Why Jesus Will Return in 1988* (based on a combination of Israel's independence in 1948 and the prophetic announcement of Jesus in Matthew 24:34). In the same vein Hal Lindsey and Carole C. Carlson together published *The Late Great Planet Earth* which sold around 30 million copies. More recently, the *Left Behind* series of fictional books co-authored by Tim LaHaye and Jerry B. Jenkins have helped to cement the teachings of Dispensationalism deep within the belief system of many believers today.

---

[256] Trench & Eberle in their book *Victorious Eschatology* make the point, "*The only earlier historical references to that doctrine have been found in the writings of Dr. John Gill (1748) and Morgan Edwards (1788).*" - location 3783 (Kindle edition)

[257] Stan Newton, *Glorious Kingdom*, location 248 (Kindle edition)

The point should not be lost on us that Dispensationalism and Rapture theory has no substantial history within church tradition, and is a relatively young theory (roughly 150 years old). Since it's early roots, the teachings of Dispensationalism have been finely nuanced and much detail has been included so that it has reached it's current form theologically known as Dispensational Premillennialism.[258] It is characterised by the following timeline of events:

- The period between Daniel's 69th and 70th week[259] is the gap we presently inhabit. For some inexplicable reason, a large gap of time (at present around 2000 years and counting…) has been inserted between those two final weeks.
- The sudden Rapture (catching up) of Christians into Heaven kickstarts Daniel's clock again taking us into his seventieth week (pre-tribulation Rapture).
- At this time, God will pour out his wrath on the world in the time known as the great Tribulation which will last for seven years (Daniel's measurement of a week is agreed by many scholars – Dispensational and otherwise – to be equal to seven years).
- During this final week, God will turn his attention to Israel and the great ingathering of the Jewish people will occur. In the midst of great suffering there will be fruitful evangelism.
- At the end of the seven years Jesus will return at his second coming.
- He will reign on earth with believers for a thousand years.
- After this period of a thousand years there will be a rebellion resulting in the final defeat of satan and the great white throne of judgment.
- This will usher in the beginning of eternity.

[258] This is the position of most of the prominent 'End Times' teachers and authors.

[259] See Daniel 9:24-27.

CLASSIC OR HISTORICAL PREMILLENNIALISM

Whilst Dispensational Premillennialism, as presented here, is very popular despite it being the 'new kid on the block,' it is by no means held by all believers. Classic or Historical Premillennialism, according to Wayne Grudem, "*has a long history from the earliest centuries onward.*"[260] According to this perspective, history will continue until we near the end when a time of great Tribulation will engulf the world. After the Tribulation, Jesus will return to Earth, satan will be bound, and all believers from throughout history will be raised to life again (first resurrection). Christ will setup his Kingdom on Earth which will be established for a thousand years. Unbelievers who survived the Tribulation will also be alive during his Earthly reign. After this time (either literal or else figuratively a long period of time) satan will be loosed and will lead a rebellion which will be crushed, leading to his final defeat and the second resurrection of the rest of the dead (unbelievers throughout history) for the final judgment. This will usher in the beginning of eternity.

POSTMILLENNIALISM

According to this view, the progress of the gospel and the church will increase to the point where we will have significant Christian influence on society and culture. This will reach a point where we will enter a 'millennial age' of peace where society will function as God wants it to. At some point after this (not necessarily a literal period of a thousand years but perhaps a period figuratively understood to mean 'a long time') Christ will return to Earth, believers and unbelievers will be raised to life, the final judgment will occur and we will enter our eternal state.

[260] Wayne Grudem, *Systematic Theology*, p.1111

PARTIAL PRETERISM

Partial preterism is the theological position that most accurately describes what I believe about the End Times. In this view the prophecies of Matthew 24 and part of the book of Revelation have already been fulfilled, whilst some parts still await fulfilment. This very loose description (which parts have been fulfilled, which parts are still awaiting fulfilment?) have led to diversity amongst those who hold to the partial preterism model. However, all agree that:

- Jesus is Lord here and now
- The Kingdom will continue to advance albeit with opposition
- The people of God will rise victoriously, in humility, maturity, unity, and power as that day approaches
- In the end, God will make all things new rather than destroy the Earth, uniting Heaven and Earth

FULL PRETERISM

Full preterism is similar to the partial perspective with the exception that those who hold to this position believe all the prophecies of Matthew 24 and Revelation have already been fulfilled in history past.

CHAPTER THIRTY-TWO

Bibliography

BOOKS

Adam Clarke's Commentary on Matthew **Adam Clarke**

Victorious Eschatology **Harold Eberle and Martin Trench**

Reading Revelation Responsibly **Michael Gorman**

Systematic Theology **Wayne Grudem**

The Wars of the Jews **Josephus**

Breakthrough: Discovering the Kingdom **Derek Morphew**

Glorious Kingdom **Stan Newton**

Colossians Remixed: Subverting the Empire **Brian Walsh and Sylvia Keesmaat**

The Art of Revelation **Jonathan Welton**

Raptureless: An Optimistic Guide to the End of the World **Jonathan Welton**

Wesley's explanatory notes on the New Testament **John Wesley**

New Testament and the People of God **N.T. Wright**

Surprised by Hope **Tom Wright**

Revelation for Everyone **Tom Wright**

Matthew for Everyone **Tom Wright**

Paul for Everyone: Galatians and Thessalonians **Tom Wright**

Paul and Caesar: A New Reading of Romans **Tom Wright** (http://ntwrightpage.com/2016/07/12/paul-and-caesar-a-new-reading-of-romans/)

Olive Tree Enhanced Strong's Dictionary (electronic version)

WEBSITES

http://www.ntwrightpage.com

http://www.preteristarchive.com